Hollywood Hybrids

D1198308

Genre and Beyond
A Film Studies Series
Series Editor: Leonard Leff, Oklahoma State University

Genre and Beyond offers fresh perspectives on conceptions of film as well as cinema's role in a changing world. Books in the series explore often overlooked or unconventional genres as well as more traditional themes. These engaging texts have the rigor that scholars demand and the creativity and accessibility that students and interested readers expect.

Titles in the Series

Cinematic Shakespeare
Michael Anderegg

Black Lenses, Black Voices: African American Film Now
Mark A. Reid

High Comedy in American Movies:
Class and Humor from the 1920s to the Present
Steve Vineberg

Queer Images: Homosexuality in American Film
Harry M. Benshoff and Sean Griffin

Now a Major Motion Picture: Film Adaptations of Literature and Drama
Christine Geraghty

Hollywood Hybrids: Mixing Genres in Contemporary Films
Ira Jaffe

Forthcoming in the Series

The Documentary Imagination
Seth Feldman

Hollywood Hybrids

Mixing Genres in Contemporary Films

IRA JAFFE

ROWMAN & LITTLEFIELD PUBLISHERS, INC.
Lanham • Boulder • New York • Toronto • Plymouth, UK

ROWMAN & LITTLEFIELD PUBLISHERS, INC.

Published in the United States of America
by Rowman & Littlefield Publishers, Inc.
A wholly owned subsidary of The Rowman & Littlefield Publishing Group, Inc.
4501 Forbes Boulevard, Suite 200, Lanham, Maryland 20706
www.rowmanlittlefield.com

Estover Road, Plymouth PL6 7PY, United Kingdom

Copyright © 2008 by Rowman & Littlefield Publishers, Inc.

All rights reserved. No part of this publication may be reproduced, stored in a
retrieval system, or transmitted in any form or by any means, electronic, mechanical,
photocopying, recording, or otherwise, without the prior permission of the publisher.

British Library Cataloguing in Publication Information Available

Library of Congress Cataloging-in-Publication Data
Jaffe, Ira
    Hollywood hybrids : mixing genres in contemporary films / Ira Jaffe.
        p. cm. — (Genre and beyond)
    Includes bibliographical references and index.
    ISBN-13: 978-0-7425-3950-1 (cloth : alk. paper)
    ISBN-10: 0-7425-3950-4 (cloth : alk. paper)
    ISBN-13: 978-0-7425-3951-8 (pbk. : alk. paper)
    ISBN-10: 0-7425-3951-2 (pbk. : alk. paper)
    1. Film genres—United States. 2. Motion pictures—United States. I. Title.
PN1993.5.U6J23 2008
791.43'60973—dc22

                                                                          2007028812

Printed in the United States of America

∞™ The paper used in this publication meets the minimum requirements of American
National Standard for Information Sciences—Permanence of Paper for Printed Library
Materials, ANSI/NISO Z39.48-1992.

In memory of my friends

Harry Nadler

Gus Blaisdell

Contents

Acknowledgments

My thanks to the editors affiliated with Rowman & Littlefield who have guided this book to completion for the series "Beyond Genre." Leonard Leff, series editor, invited me to contribute and provided vital insights and suggestions. Acquisitions editor Brenda Hadenfeldt kept the project moving, commented astutely on the text, and led the search for the book's title. Also effective and gracious in their respective roles have been assistant editor Bess Vanrenen and production editor Alden Perkins.

Among the friends and acquaintances who have inspired and cared for me during my working life, I thank Joanne Wilson Jaffe, Betty Hahn, Diana Robin, Leonard Lehrer, Helen Sturges Nadler, Peter Walch, Charlene McDermott, Elen Feinberg, Louise Lennihan, Eric Patrick, Reuben Hersh, David Vogel, Nancy Morrison, and Richard Rubin. Not least I thank Joan Bybee, my wife—conservation rancher, pianist, homemaker, world-renowned linguistics scholar, and caring partner who expands my horizons daily (and who I will ask to review these acknowledgments). Joan's mother, Elizabeth, died as I planned this book; my mother, Lillie, died as I wrote it. We salute them both.

Introduction

As he lowers the coffin door and prepares to bury her alive, Budd (Michael Madsen) tells The Bride (Uma Thurman), "This is for breakin' my brother's heart." But moments earlier in *Kill Bill Vol. 2* (2004), on a rare visit to Budd's trailer home in the desert, his brother Bill (David Carradine) says that Budd has been angry with him for years, and their scene ends with no apparent change of feeling. Along with anger, does Budd feel more warmth and affection for Bill than he admits? He informs Bill that for just $250 he has hocked the invaluable Hattori Hanzo sword Bill gave him, yet The Bride (a.k.a. Beatrix Kiddo) will come upon the sword in Budd's trailer later in the movie as she battles Elle Driver (Daryl Hannah). Perhaps in anger Budd disowns his affection for Bill much as he does the sword that presumably attests to his brother's love and to the bonds they share. Characters in both parts of *Kill Bill* often harbor not simply mixed feelings and instincts, but primal, clashing ones that are resolved only in violent killing. Thus, even though he seems caring when he warns Budd that Beatrix is on her way to kill him, Bill presides—albeit at a distance—over his brother's murder by the venomous Black Mamba snake deployed by Elle Driver.

KILL BILL: MIXED FEELINGS

Tarantino's films have been criticized for lacking emotional range and for reveling in graphic violence that leaves civilized spectators feeling empty, angry,

1

and numb.[1] Yet Budd as well as other Tarantino characters suggest a range of emotion sufficient to evoke a broader audience response. In a further instance of Budd's sensitivity, brutish though he may be, he asks Elle Driver whether she feels primarily regret or relief over the apparent defeat of her old enemy Beatrix, whom she has long respected as well as despised. Earlier in the film, Budd's emotion is palpable as he resigns himself to humiliation at the tavern where he works as a bouncer and doubles as a janitor; later, he sounds an oddly intimate, tender note as he tells Beatrix, tied up in the coffin, to stop struggling lest she oblige him to spray mace in her eyes.

Kill Bill's emotional range and incongruity probably peak in the final chapter, "Face to Face," as Bill and Beatrix, not merely enemies, warriors, and former lovers, but parents of the child Bibi, converse directly for the first time since Bill shot The Bride almost five years earlier, as depicted in the inaugural scene of *Vol. 1* (2003) and reprised at the start of *Vol. 2*. Beatrix has had no inkling that her baby survived when Bill fired into her pregnant body at the rehearsal at the Twin Pines chapel for her marriage to another man. She has not realized she is a mother, and that the man she fervently seeks to kill is Bibi's father instead of Bibi's killer. In Mexico for the final chapter, she finds that Bill makes Bibi serenely happy in their bounteous hacienda by the sea, though he does authorize and perhaps direct Bibi to aim a toy gun at her mother when Beatrix, brandishing a real one, charges into their paradise. Bill softly tells Bibi as Beatrix appears, "Bang-bang, she got us baby. I'm dying," whereupon Bibi chimes in, "I'm dying," and both father and daughter fall to the ground. Then Bibi rises, aims her gun at her mother, and says, "Bang-bang." Bill decrees, "You're dead mommy. So die," and Beatrix compliantly falls. Thus begins this family's game reunion.

Contrary feelings continue to roil each parent for the remainder of "Face to Face." Beatrix's tearful ecstasy when she rises from her mock death to lift Bibi to her lips does not keep her from firing at Bill a look of uncompromising, incredulous hate. He in turn shortly suggests that contrary feelings may be part of her identity, as of his: "I think you would have been a wonderful mother. But you are a killer." Indeed, she was not only his lover—the lover of a killer who has become a loving father—but also a member of his band of assassins, hitting targets all over the world for vast sums of money. She explains she wanted her daughter "to be born with a clean slate," to which Bill replies that Beatrix could not have been happy, nor true to herself, working in a record shop in El Paso alongside the pallid man she chose to marry after discovering she was pregnant. Injected with truth serum from a dart Bill shoots into her thigh, Beatrix regretfully agrees. The clean slate—purity, innocence—was not in the cards.

The fact that *Kill Bill* foregrounds divided identity and warring instincts and emotions does not alone make it a major instance of hybrid cinema. Yet more distinctive are its abrupt shifts of tone, style, and generic reference, often cited in discussions of the film. In the still night after Bibi falls asleep, Bill and Beatrix quietly compare their perspectives on events leading up to the fatal wedding rehearsal: Beatrix's early hope for their baby; her decision to run away; Bill's conclusion after she vanished that she was dead; his grief and anguish; his search for her killers; his broken-hearted discovery of the truth. Suddenly, though, their temperate, soulful exchange of confidences and confessions erupts into physical combat. Bill has shot bullets and darts at Beatrix earlier in the chapter. Now Bibi's reunited parents, emotionally closer to each other than to any other adult in the world, shift to samurai swords and kung fu for their climactic duel. Beatrix inflicts the "deadliest blow in all of martial arts"; spaghetti-Western music trumpets both doom and triumph in the succulent Mexican night; Bill stands up, marks five paces, and drops dead for real.

Shifts of tone, style, and generic reference in *Kill Bill* are often more radical than in this penultimate scene of the film. In *Vol. 1*, for instance, The Bride, having magically arisen from her four-year coma and escaped by wheelchair from the hospital in which she was repeatedly raped, lies flat in a van ("pussy wagon" inscribed on its rear doors) in the hospital garage, vainly attempting to revive feeling and movement in her paralyzed toes and feet. Bill's squad of assassins who performed the massacre at the wedding rehearsal appear in her mind's eye, first as a still photograph, then as a live tableau. Voice-over, The Bride focuses on O-Ren Ishii (Lucy Liu), a Japanese-Chinese-American squad member who, with Bill's help after the massacre, has become "queen of the Tokyo underworld." As Beatrix speaks of O-Ren's woeful childhood, *Kill Bill* shifts from live action to Japanese *anime*, which depicts O-Ren at age nine under a bed helplessly watching a Yakuza boss rape her mother and kill both her parents; then the *anime* depicts the vengeful O-Ren two years later murdering the Yakuza boss, a pederast, while having sex with him. Geysers of blood, along with horror, pity, and grief, flood the scene. At moments, as if to imply that O-Ren's physical and emotional traumas defy words, figurative images give way to blank sheets of color. All that O-Ren endures, and all she nonetheless achieves, cannot help but inspire Beatrix as she struggles to get well. The underworld queen offers a further incentive in that Beatrix must recover in order to kill her for having participated in the massacre at the church. When, following the *anime*, live action returns, Beatrix, still in the van, says to herself, "Wiggle your big toe," and her command works.

Although *Kill Bill* does not show Beatrix specifically learning the lethal "exploding heart" technique she employs against Bill at the end of the film, in the chapter titled "The Cruel Tutelage of Pai Mei," *Kill Bill Vol. 2* describes her introduction to martial arts. Moreover, as in the rendering of O-Ren's childhood, changes in cinematic style, tone, and generic reference mark Beatrix's kung fu initiation. Further, the prelude to "The Cruel Tutelage of Pai Mei" itself entails changes of tone, style, and generic reference: First the screen goes black, as Beatrix's coffin is lowered into the grave and covered with earth, following Budd's statement that she broke Bill's heart. As light returns, from a flashlight Budd has given Beatrix, the normal range of color above ground in the cemetery yields to high-contrast black-and-white, like that in the images of Beatrix's face on the floor at the abortive wedding rehearsal as Bill shot her. Again in the coffin—as in the "Pussy Wagon" where she invoked O-Ren— Beatrix is on her back, immobilized, her hands and feet now bound with rope; and again she invokes a character from her past, in this case Pai Mei, in order to break free. From Beatrix's black-and-white anguish, however, the film cuts directly not to her lessons with Pai Mei, but to a relaxed, radiant Beatrix, bathed in the colorful glow of a campfire at night, smiling adoringly at Bill as he plays the flute and tells her the tale of Pai Mei's priestly, martial ascent. At the end of this perfect bedtime story, Beatrix prepares for a sumptuous sleep. Only then does *Kill Bill* shift to Pai Mei's harsh habitat, including its steep, endless stone stairway, to describe Beatrix's arduous instruction.

Cinematic style shifts along with action and setting for Beatrix's schooling. In this new sequence, Pai Mei's leaps and levitations defy gravity, and Hong Kong-style snap-zooms in and out[2] supplant the more stable, stationary look of the campfire scene. Furthermore, color, focus, light, and texture deteriorate in the new sequence—as Tarantino intended. *Kill Bill*'s cinematographer, Robert Richardson, states, "Quentin wanted to replicate the visual generation loss in these old kung fu films—the scratches, the higher-than-normal contrast." Consequently, according to the *American Cinematographer*, Richardson "began by capturing the action on contrasty Kodachrome color-reversal stock. He processed that normally, struck an internegative from the print and then struck an interpositive from *that*, and so on." Adds Richardson: "We just kept making dupes and prints back and forth until Quentin was happy with the look."[3]

SUBVERTING AND UPENDING GENERIC EXPECTATIONS

It's worth reiterating that this look Richardson cites is but one of several in *Kill Bill*—which, like Tarantino's *Pulp Fiction* (1994) and other work, blends various genres that diverge in style and appearance as they depict diverse moods and actions. Richardson underscores the quest for such differences in *Kill Bill*: "One of the first statements Quentin made was that he wanted each chapter of the script to feel like a reel from a different film. He wanted to move in and out of the various signature styles of all these genres—Western, melodrama, thriller, horror. He had an absolute knowledge of what he wanted each sequence to look like."[4] A commonplace about Tarantino advanced by co-workers like Richardson, as well as by interviewers, reviewers, critics, and the director himself, is that Tarantino, as moviegoer *and* filmmaker, is a genre omnivore. As evidence that ". . . he likes nearly everything," a 2003 *New Yorker* profile lists nearly 30 of his favorite film types and genres, many of which are invoked in *Kill Bill*: "gangster movies . . . action movies . . . men-on-a-mission movies . . . grindhouse, sexploitation, blaxploitation, kung fu, silent, New Wave . . . animé, animation, sci-fi . . . horror . . . Westerns, spaghetti Westerns, musicals . . . thrillers, fantasies, epics, and romances."[5] One might add "family melodrama" in the case of *Kill Bill*, since tensions linked to lost children, lost parents, and lost love seethe everywhere in the film. Moreover, characters like Budd, O-Ren, Elle Driver, and even Karen, who arrives to assassinate Beatrix after Beatrix discovers she is pregnant, know each other almost too well. Joined by memories of past intimacies, they resemble a demonic family exploding.[6]

In calling attention over the years to his enthusiasm for multiple genres, Tarantino has underscored a further dimension of his films: he seeks not merely to quote and allude to an array of genres, but also to subvert them and upend his audience's generic expectations. In the *New Yorker* profile he states that each of his movies acknowledges that "I'm inside of a genre, or I'm subverting a genre."[7] Such subversion typically involves juxtaposing diverse generic elements in odd or surprising ways, as well as inserting incongruous and disorienting events that are not explained or resolved in the logical manner of classical narrative. He states in a 1994 interview, "My favorite musical sequences have always been in Godard [French filmmaker Jean-Luc Godard], because they just come out of nowhere."[8] Similarly, Tarantino exults that Christopher Walken's intense monologue detailing the history of the gold watch in *Pulp Fiction* provokes the audience to ask, "What the fuck did that have to do with anything?"[9] Contrasting fiction to everyday life a bit later in the interview, Tarantino again celebrates the disruption of genre: "The idea is to take genre characters and put them in real-life situations and make them live by real-life rules. In normal movies, they're too busy telling the plot to have guns go off accidentally and kill someone we don't give a damn about. But it happens. . . ."[10]

As indicated above, aside from their heavy violence, Tarantino's films such as *Kill Bill* have been criticized as hermetic events, busily juggling genres while excluding real life. But Tarantino suggests that his films do admit reality, if only to subvert genre and add to each film's jarring mix of tones, styles, and generic references. Hybrid cinema is the label I propose for such odd mixtures, whether directed by Tarantino or other filmmakers, such as Pedro Almodóvar, Stephen Chow, David Lynch, Todd Haynes, and Joel and Ethan Coen. In these directors' hybrid works, the prominence of any one genre may vary from one moment to the next in a particular film. Now comedy may rule, then melodrama, farce, tragedy, horror, sci-fi, kung fu, film noir, or the Western; now realism, then surrealism or expressionism. Possibly hybrid films are inherently subversive, since in mingling genres and styles instead of keeping them separate, these films choose heterogeneity over homogeneity, contamination over purity. Further, as these films embrace incongruity and incidents that "just come out of nowhere," they verge on disorder and chaos. They may be regarded as not just disorienting, but as destructive and nihilistic, which may support the notion that genre quotation, mimicry, mingling, and parody signal an exhaustion of creative energy—an inability to conceive much that is new or original, to think or feel deeply, to break through genre discourses to life itself. A more positive spin, though, might stress that unsettling, disorderly, and absurdist aspects of hybrid cinema faithfully reflect as well as influence contemporary life. Moreover, genres get established precisely because they speak to major human concerns and do make contact with life. But along with the times they must change, or undergo revision, for that contact to remain vibrant, which is where the recombinant meddling and foolery of hybrid cinema come in.

At its best this cinema might embrace the values Salman Rushdie has ascribed to *The Satanic Verses,* his novel that prompted a fatwa against his life. The book "celebrates hybridity, impurity, intermingling, the transformation that comes of new and unexpected combinations of human beings, cultures, ideas, politics, movies, songs," states Rushdie. "It rejoices in mongrelisation and fears the absolutism of the Pure. Melange, hotch-potch, a bit of this and a bit of that is how newness enters the world."[11] Whether hybrid cinema betokens the kind of birth and renewal Rushdie indicates, or a withdrawal from life, a deadening of thought and feeling, such cinema has become increasingly prominent in Hollywood and elsewhere in the last quarter of a century. Yet hybrid form is nothing new in film history or in the history of art and culture generally. The following pages review aspects of this historical context that anticipate recent hybrid cinema.

UNITY AND DIVERSITY

In his introduction to *Movies,* a collection of his essays that begins with praise for action films by Hollywood directors such as Howard Hawks and Raoul Walsh, critic Manny Farber pauses to praise French filmmaker Jean-Luc Godard's *Weekend* (1967) for its diversity of form and tone. Almost every segment of this film appears to follow "a different stylistic format," says Farber, yet overall the film possesses strong stylistic unity.[12] Whether or not Farber is right about *Weekend,* and I believe for the most part he is, the phenomenon he points to—diverse stylistic and generic impulses converging in films of surprising unity—constitutes, as I have indicated, the principal interest of *Hollywood Hybrids: Mixing Genres in Contemporary Films.*

Most movies are diverse in their materials, as they consist of sounds and images initially recorded in disjoint circumstances but finally incorporated into logical and natural continuums. Even individual shots in early films such as Georges Méliès's *Trip to the Moon* (1902) and E.S. Porter's *Life of an American Fireman* (1902) and *The Great Train Robbery* (1903) incorporated diverse elements and tactics, including miniatures, matte paintings, superimpositions, and shifts in the pro-filmic subject during suspensions of the celluloid's motion through the camera. More recently, images in science fiction and other films have frequently wedded live action to computer-generated effects.

Further, as in the convergence of melodrama, dream, and documentary in *Life of an American Fireman*, and of comedy, dance, and science fiction in *Trip to the Moon*, diversity of style often has accompanied the undisguised use of diverse materials. At the dawn of commercial cinema, such diversity of style within individual films was compatible with entire programs of short films of disparate events and styles, which perhaps emulated the variety of live performances in vaudeville and the circus that had captivated audiences then turning to film. But increasingly the goal in Hollywood after the start of the twentieth century was to limit diversity of style (if not of material), as it might disrupt the narrative flow and illusion of reality presumably preferred by increasingly affluent filmgoers courted by the film industry. By 1915, when Cecil B. DeMille's *The Cheat* and D.W. Griffith's *The Birth of a Nation* appeared, the ideal had shifted more decisively toward greater homogeneity: Hollywood was aiming for feature-length films distinguished by unity, clarity, and logical flow and continuity—key attributes of the classic Hollywood narrative.

In depicting four distinct periods of human history ranging from ancient Babylon to modern New York, Griffith's *Intolerance* (1916) possibly sustained a more disjunctive or heterogeneous concept of what a film might be. But stylistic and generic differences—pertaining, for example, to settings, actions, and costumes—that distinguished the four interwoven stories in this film were overridden by the hatred, violence, and bombast that spread almost monotonously across all of them. Fresh rationale and energy for generating and sustaining exceptional juxtapositions of images and styles arose amid the post-war ferment and experimentation in the USSR and Europe in the 1920s.

Soviet Filmmakers and Dissonance

After the Bolshevik revolution of 1917, vanguard Soviet filmmakers such as Sergei Eisenstein, Dziga Vertov, and Alexandre Dovzhenko frequently punctured conventional storytelling and stylistic uniformity with surprise, dissonance, and shock. Since conflict for Eisenstein was central to art as well as to life, history, and science, he often framed and juxtaposed shots in ways that promoted visual and conceptual discrepancy and collision. The nondiegetic (i.e., drawn from outside the film's story) burst of religious images ranging from a Baroque Christ to an Eskimo idol that confronted the anti-revolutionary General Kornilov in *October* (1927–28) constituted but one flagrant instance of Eisenstein's passion for creating puzzling montages intended to provoke spectators to see, think, and feel in new ways about religion, politics, and virtually every other major aspect of their experience.

Eisenstein's quest for the new, like that of his fellow filmmakers, was linked to the conviction that the cinema was a universal language and a burgeoning art form capable of enhancing human freedom and equality. His artistic strategy in the 1920s for transforming his audience's vision, thought, and feeling entailed liberating the cinema from stylistic and narrative constraints. In stating the premises of intellectual montage that spurred him to insert the religious images in *October* and that informed his most far-reaching strategies for representing and stimulating thought processes as well as emotions, he called for "liberation of the whole action from the definition of time and space."[13] Vertov, who capped the 1920s with his magisterial *The Man with a Movie Camera* (1929), pursued a similar end. Mobilized and empowered by both the movie camera and the tools of editing, he claimed to break "free of the limits of time and space" in *The Man with a Movie Camera*, putting "together any given points in the universe, no matter where I've recorded them."[14] Thereby he was helping to create, he added, a "new, perfect man"—a new mass hero, film spectator, and filmmaker, a newly unbound citizen.[15]

Goals of liberation from stylistic and narrative norms, and from spatiotemporal limits, engendered stylistic and generic diversity, if not always the spectator's transformation, in several Soviet films of the 1920s prior to socialist realism's stifling of experimentation in the next decade. Eisenstein's first feature, *Strike* (1924), for example, was a mélange of documentary, essay, propaganda, fiction, satire, and tragedy. In this exhilarating yet disorienting film, editing deliberately left unclear how one space or locale related to another. Moreover, naturalistic acting often collided with grotesque performances drawn from the Factory of the Eccentric Actor. There was also a wealth of special effects, including reversals of motion, transformations of still photographs into motion pictures, and magical dissolves of winsome capitalist spies into animals and birds, all evoking the optical wit and anarchy of Mack Sennett, Buster Keaton, and Méliès.

Yet more perplexing than *Strike* to many observers was the stylistic mix that surfaced in Dovzhenko's first feature *Zvenigora* (1927). Implored by its anxious, baffled financial backers to assess the film, Eisenstein, accompanied by his respected colleague V. I. Pudovkin, declared Dovzhenko to be a major new artist and *Zvenigora* to be a marvelous if incomprehensible work—an "astonishing mixture of reality with a profoundly poetic imagination. Quite modern and mythological at the same time."[16] Thus, incongruity and odd stylistic mixtures tended to inspire Eisenstein and some of his fellow artists, rather than put them off.

Dadaist and Surrealist Filmmakers and the Irrational

Passion for unlikely convergences of images, styles, and ideas during the 1920s was even more characteristic of Dadaist and Surrealist artists in France and elsewhere in Europe, who tended to celebrate random and irrational aspects of life and art far more than the Soviets did. If the Soviets applauded reason, science, materialism, and the machine—creeds and means for building new societies, Dadaist filmmakers like Man Ray (*Return to Reason*, 1921) and René Clair (*Entr'acte*, 1924) were propelled by the experience of World War I to foreground illogical, destructive aspects of human conduct; and Surrealists like Luis Buñuel and Salvador Dalí were drawn to dreams, imagination, and the unconscious, realms highlighted by Sigmund Freud and other exponents of psychoanalysis in the first decades of the twentieth century. Buñuel, who with Dalí created *Un Chien andalou* (1929), perhaps the most famous Surrealist film, later remarked that this work derived from "an encounter between two dreams"—Dalí's of a "hand crawling with ants" and Buñuel's of a "tapering cloud" that "sliced the moon in half, like a razor blade slicing through an eye"—both graphically rendered in their film.[17] A less violent encounter often cited as exemplary of Surrealism was that between an umbrella and a sewing machine on a dissecting table. In any case, as Buñuel notes in his autobiography, he and Dalí agreed that in *Un Chien andalou* "no idea or image that might lend itself to a rational explanation of any kind would be accepted. We had to open all doors to the irrational and keep only those images that surprised us, without trying to explain why."[18]

Whereas Eisenstein and Vertov often sought to explain and justify in their writings the unusual juxtapositions that occurred in their films, Surrealists and Dadaists preferred stressing the absence and impossibility of explanation, as if to underscore the irreparability of the disjunctions and contradictions that distinguished their cinema. Further, at least until André Breton, author of the Surrealist Manifesto in 1924, became a communist five years later, Surrealists and Dadaists were less likely than the Soviets to link their films and other art to constructive political purposes. Indeed, more than a whiff of nihilism inflected Buñuel's claim that *Un Chien andalou* was a passionate call to murder. Nonetheless, Surrealist and Dadaist films shared with those of the Soviets a determination to free human consciousness and conduct from repressive cultural, social, and political norms. As Buñuel remarked, Surrealism was a moral as well as poetic movement.[19]

Cinematic Experimentation in the Sixties

Both outrage at repression and the drive to enlarge human awareness, expression, and justice also fueled cinematic experiment in the 1960s, perhaps the next great era of unusual stylistic and generic encounters at the periphery of commercial cinema. Spared global war and economic depression, but not cultural and sociopolitical crisis, this era witnessed cinematic regeneration on multiple fronts, including the U.S. avant-garde and new waves in Europe, Japan, and Latin America.

In *A Movie* (1958), *Report* (1964), and other films, Bruce Conner in the U.S. created fast-paced collages comprised of excerpts from documentaries, fiction films, commercials, educational films, and television news highlighting events and cultural values stretching from World War I to the assassination of President John F. Kennedy. Often appearing in no obvious temporal or logical order, the events depicted in Conner's kinetic collages seemed simultaneous as well as enigmatic. An array of human characters, animals, objects, and places in these films invoked diverse generic and stylistic impulses from film and television history. There were cowboys and Indians, athletes and assassins, elephants and refrigerators, jungles and cities, soldiers and mad scientists, bullfighters and financial secretaries, Popes and Presidents, smiling Americans and starving Africans. Ironic, turbulent streams of consciousness, Conner's films sounded alarms against violence, the media, capitalism, and inequality, and were further unified by repeated convergences of play and disaster, comedy and tragedy, fantasy and reality, love and death.

Another avant-garde U.S. filmmaker whose work presaged wider use of mixed generic and stylistic signals in Hollywood and elsewhere was Stan Brakhage, hailed by Princeton University film historian P. Adams Sitney as the "preeminent" film artist of the twentieth century when he died in March 2003.[20] In *Dog Star Man* (1961–64), perhaps his most renowned work, Brakhage painted and scrawled over "live-action" images, and juxtaposed footage he had shot himself (and in which he and members of his family appeared) with stock

scientific footage and other found images. Hence at a given moment the multiple layers of superimposition in *Dog Star Man* might encompass abstract
painting in motion, intimacies of the young family at home, and distant heav-
ens recorded at scientific observatories.

However, perhaps Brakhage's primary contribution to hybrid cinema, or to
the conjoining of diverse stylistic and generic impulses, involved aspects of his
films that might be considered purist. Like other devisers of unusual juxtapositions, he aspired to liberate and transform human vision, a goal that for him
entailed representing and restoring something like original seeing—the free
and abundant flux of the newborn child's untutored sight. He sought to rein-
state natural vision in place of restrictive habits that he traced back to Renaissance rules of linear perspective adopted by Leon Battista Alberti and other
Western European painters. In *Metaphors on Vision*, which he wrote while he
made *Dog Star Man*, Brakhage asserted that contrary to Renaissance perspective, the actual world of sight is ever shifting, pulsing, blurred, and fragmented; ever exceeding the confines of neat, tightly knit stories; and always a
fusion of external stimuli and inner events such as memories, fantasies, and
remnants of dreams and closed-eye images. While noting that Renaissance
rules continued to shape contemporary notions of how the world looked—
and of how cameras, lenses, and editing should be designed and deployed in
order to yield that look—Brakhage resolved to manipulate film technology so
as to project what he considered true seeing on the screen. His films, which he
often described as documentaries about seeing, rejected norms of movie vision like sharp focus, deep space, tripod steadiness, and even legibility. The dynamic result bore greater resemblance to American Abstract Expressionist
painting of the late 1940s and early '50s—to work by Jackson Pollock and
Dutch-born Willem de Kooning, for example—than to either Renaissance
painting or the typical product of industrial movie studios in Hollywood and
elsewhere. In addition, Brakhage's films were silent, partly because he believed
that music, words, and other sounds disturbed the visual concentration and
learning his films required.

Thus, more significant than the mix of different types of footage in
Brakhage's films was his overall notion of seeing, which rejected the norms of
industrial vision. Brakhage's films did not merely criticize visual and narrative
conventions hostile to stylistic and generic diversity and to other forms of dis-
junction and disorientation in the cinema. Rather, his films presented a grand

monly identified with mise-en-scène or the unedited scene in front of the camera, he has observed, "montage . . . both denies and prepares the way for . . . *mise en scène*: the two are interdependent."[22] Also interdependent, rather than merely contrasting, in his view are apparent antinomies such as documentary and fiction, real and imaginary, natural and manipulated. Citing cinema's beginnings, he has found the theatrical magic of Méliès and the physical objectivity of the Lumières complementary to one another: while Méliès located ordinary elements within the extraordinary, the Lumières underscored the extraordinary in the everyday. Godard has stated he would like to be "in charge of the French newsreel services,"[23] and also has compared his films to newspapers. As in a newspaper, he has said, "everything should be put into a film. . . ."[24] In films as well as newspapers, "It's all there. And it's all mixed up."[25] He has considered his method a blend of further inclinations as well: "I think of myself as an essayist, producing essays in novel form, or novels in essay form: only instead of writing, I film them."[26]

In keeping with Godard's tendency to locate models and parallels to his work outside cinema history, his films refer to diverse artistic and cultural media in addition to other films. *Weekend*, the film highlighted by Farber, cites not only numerous cinematic works representing diverse genres—such as *Potemkin* (1925, Sergei Eisenstein), *The Searchers* (1957, John Ford), *Johnny Guitar* (1954, Nicholas Ray), *It Happened One Night* (1934, Frank Capra), and *Gösta Berling* (1924, Mauritz Stiller)—but also music by Mozart and the Beatles and Freud's *Totem and Taboo* (1912). *Weekend* also presents a character identified as Emily Brontë, the British poet and author of *Wuthering Heights* (1848); after she asks the two primary characters whether they seek "poetical or concrete information,"[27] they set her on fire. Further, the film resurrects Louis Antoine Leon de Saint-Just, a French revolutionary leader guillotined in 1794, played here by Jean-Pierre Léaud, the same who first won fame as the neglected boy in *The 400 Blows* (1959, François Truffaut), which like *Breathless* helped inaugurate the French New Wave.

An intimate of Robespierre often identified with the onset of the Reign of Terror, Saint-Just with book in hand rails in Godard's film about the treacherous triumph of wealth and violence over justice and fellow feeling, presumably in the present as well as in the past: "I see only constitutions which are backed by gold, pride and blood and nowhere do I see . . . gentle humanity . . . the fairness and moderation which ought to form the basis of the social treaty."[28] On the relationship between his films and society, Godard has remarked, "All of my films have been reports on the state of the nation . . . treated in a personal manner perhaps"[29]—and for "nation" he might have said "world." The invocations of diverse cultural stances and voices in his films almost certainly broaden the perspective and authority of his reports on modern life, including its brutality.

Moreover, the references in Godard's films to other films representing various genres suggest not only his personal take or report on film history, but also his intention to transform cinematic conventions in keeping with changes in modern life. Of his first film, *Breathless*, he famously said, "What I wanted was to take a conventional story and remake, but differently, everything the cinema had done."[30] He added that he wanted to break the rules and "show that anything goes."[31] At the outset, then, he raised prospects of anarchy. But what would replace the conventions of character and story he intended to abandon? Would Godard merely offer perplexing cultural and cinematic quotations and allusions? Disorienting shifts and clashes of stylistic and generic direction? Jarring jump cuts and ellipses?

While the answer would vary from film to film, possibly the passion for poetry, justice, and gentle humanity evinced by Brontë and Saint-Just in *Weekend* propels much of Godard's work, knitting together the diverse stylistic strands and patterns mentioned by Manny Farber. As indicated above, such stylistic and generic diversity is hardly limited to *Weekend*, the film Farber singled out, but typifies most of Godard's work, reflecting his vision of modern life's fragmentation, violence, and disarray, as well as his determination to reshape the cinema. Yet the diversity in *Weekend*, when compared to Godard's other work, seems particularly expansive and engaging as well as aggressive. Not only do essay, novel, and news report intermingle in this film, but also past and present, as well as dream, fantasy, and reality. Further, *Weekend*'s generic diversity incorporates aspects of melodrama, tragedy, comedy, satire, slapstick, farce, fantasy, horror, film noir, political cinema, documentary, militant propaganda, and even science fiction.

Weekend's characters are as unstable and blurred, and its events as ambiguous, as its generic modes. One moment Corinne's husband Roland joins her in renouncing their shared ignorance and brutality, and the next, calling her an idiot, tells her to lie down on the road and part her legs to hitch a ride. Actors play more than one character, or depart from their roles in other ways. After Corinne and her lover plot to kill her husband in the first scene (while her husband plots *her* death), she appears in the next scene as her lover's psychiatric patient, reporting to him an unusual erotic experience. "Did all this really happen?" he finally asks at the end of her lengthy account, or was it just a nightmare?[32] Her reply that she doesn't really know suggests the indeterminateness of events as well as of characters that persists throughout the film. Who is Joseph Balsamo, the individual identifying himself as the Son of God and Alexandre Dumas as he descends upon Corinne and Roland in their automobile en route to her parents' home and magically plucks a wiggling rabbit from under the dashboard? (There *was* in the eighteenth century a well-known Italian imposter named Giuseppe Balsamo.) What shall we make of Jean-Pierre Léaud portraying not only Saint-Just but also, moments later, a young man in modern dress "calling out in the emptiness" from a rural phone booth?[33] And, does the sublime yet unlikely performance of a Mozart sonata on a grand piano in a farmyard "really happen"?

Although, as indicated above, Godard's role was central in the expanded mixing and shifting of generic and stylistic directions that reconfigured action and character in many of the most challenging films of the '60s, he was not alone. Nagisa Oshima of Japan, perhaps most strikingly in his celebrated *Death by Hanging* (1969), was one of those who explored similar terrain. In his absurdist, sociopolitically urgent films, Oshima incorporated elements of documentary, fiction, propaganda, farce, comedy, and tragedy, and juxtaposed diverse, often contradictory images, plotlines, editing styles, and uses of the camera.

Oshima referred to the conglomerate as a "cinema of subjectivity."[34] His cinematic tactics brought to the fore not just the inner and unconscious life of the individual, but also the ideological bent of the entire society. Like feminists and other cultural critics then as now, Oshima stressed that the personal was tied to the social and political, that individual identity hinged on pervasive public assumptions about power, freedom, and justice. As he revised cinematic form, genre, and subject matter, exposing diverse levels of public and private life, he probed the psychological roots and consequences of such developments as Japanese nationalism, the persecution of Koreans and other minorities, and security agreements with the United States.

Undoubtedly Oshima sought not just to reveal greater truth, but also to alter reality. His conflicting generic and stylistic directions, along with his disorienting temporal and spatial shifts, both reflected the rich diversity of human personality and consciousness and stimulated the imagination and understanding necessary for change. Experimental Latin American films of the period comparably probed the multi-dimensionality of film and human identity in relation to historical change. The multiple nicknames society accords the main character in *The Jackal of Nahueltoro* (1969, Chile, Miguel Littín), for instance, suggest the diverse faces and traits he presents to society and that over time he discovers both within himself and in the world. Born into loss and mayhem, he undertakes in this non-linear film, as it hurtles back and forth across the span of his life, profound changes of spirit and conduct. He knows extremes of oppression, violence, and hatred, yet gains education, civility, and gentleness. As he notes in his plea to avert execution, he finally becomes a very different person. The film's style changes as well—from scenes of human commotion rendered via violent editing and a veering, hand-held camera, for instance, to decidedly quieter, more stable moments; and from realistic imagery to nondiegetic, ironic inserts.

Lucía (1968, Cuba, Humberto Solas) exhibits even sharper, more sustained stylistic and generic contrasts, invoking romance, tragedy, opera, comedy, and documentary. However, the potential for confusion and anarchy in this stylistic and generic cauldron, wherein the heroine undergoes various incarnations, is tempered by the film's division into three distinct episodes corresponding to distinct periods of Cuban history—from the war with Spain in the 1890s to the triumph of Fidel Castro and communism in the 1960s. Emerging from a different economic class but with the same name in each episode, the heroine grapples with changing historical priorities that somewhat account for—and hence "tame"—the diverse stylistic and generic currents. Another Cuban film of 1968, *Memories of Underdevelopment*, directed by Tomás Gutiérrez Alea, also poses a generic mix that shifts among different modes such as fiction and documentary. In one particularly reflexive moment, Alea himself appears in a screening room and says of his new film, "It'll be a 'collage' that'll have a bit of everything."[35] Yet much as in Littín's *Jackal of Nahueltoro*, the bits in *Memories*, including the shuttling between reality and fantasy, tend to be controlled and explained through the perspective and inner monologue of the central character. Similarly, the disparate generic impulses evident in yet another powerful Latin American film of 1968, *The Hour of the Furnaces*, made in Argentina by Fernando Solanas and Octavio Getino, seem curbed by the film's singularly militant, unambiguous viewpoint.

Thus generic and stylistic mixtures flourished in major Latin American cinema of the late '60s, but perhaps in ways that were less disjunctive, puzzling, and unsettling—less erratic, elusive, and anarchic—than in films by Godard and Oshima. Moreover, despite the attention accorded "subjectivity" by Oshima and Godard, point of view in their films was more impersonal and ironic than in the Latin American films. *Hollywood Hybrids: Mixing Genres in Contemporary Films* principally addresses cinematic mixtures closer to the model posed by Godard and Oshima—films that are enigmatic and unresolved as well as rough-edged. Exactly how the diverse generic and stylistic pieces fit together in such films isn't always easily explained. As indicated earlier, rule-breaking, untamed cinema of this sort occasionally appears merely irrational and destructive, hostile to order and structure, hostage to Dada and Surrealism. Nonetheless, Buñuel's claim that Surrealism was a moral as well as poetic movement pertains as well to the range of films and cinematic outlooks explored in this book. Given half a chance, they provoke and reward moral speculation of a most serious kind.

Intersections of Twentieth-Century Art, Music, Literature, and Film

Alea's mention, as a character in *Memories*, of "collage" that has "a bit of everything" invoked a central tendency in twentieth-century art. Just ten years prior to *Memories of Underdevelopment*, U.S. painter Robert Rauschenberg was completing *Odalisk* (1958), one of a series he called "combines" or "combine-paintings." It was composed not only of traditional elements such as oil, watercolor, and pencil, but also, as noted in a catalog description, "fabric, paper, photographs, metal, glass, electric light fixtures, dried grass, steel wool, necktie, on wood structure with four wheels, plus pillow and stuffed rooster."[36] (An eagle and an angora goat bedecked other Rauschenberg combines of the period.) As significant as the diversity of physical materials that constituted *Odalisk* was the variety of human activity thereby evoked. High and low art converged, as well as painting and sculpture, Abstract Expressionism and Pop Art, public and private realms, handsome and ugly things, sublimity and vulgarity. "This is the artist of American democracy," declared one critic, "yearningly faithful to its clamor, its contradictions, its hope and its enormous demotic freedom. . . ."[37]

Picasso, Braque, and other visual artists early in the twentieth century incorporated everyday materials in many of their works, such as Picasso's *Still Life with Chair Caning* (1912), but Rauschenberg packed in more of the motley real as well as more emblems of popular culture, yielding an effect that was messier and more boisterous. Yet probably this effect was no more jolting than the hybrid sensations evoked previously by Picasso and other creators of Cubism without the incorporation of real or mundane materials. For instance, more than the other nude forms in Picasso's celebrated *Les Demoiselles d'Avignon* (1907), a precursor of Cubism, the contorted figure in the lower right seems rendered from multiple angles; an amalgam of front, back, and side views, her beauty exists apart, as if in conflict with itself, in a realm more horrific than the rest of the composition. Further, just as hybrid visual expression could proceed without infusions of diverse physical materials, hybrid form in music by such composers as Charles Ives and Virgil Thomson advanced in the 1920s without non-musical elements, which awaited the arrival of later avant-garde figures like Edgard Varèse and John Cage.

Rauschenberg's combines appeared in the wake of parallel experiments in music by Cage, who inspired various visual artists including Rauschenberg and—in the 1980s—Jean-Michel Basquiat. Perhaps most notoriously in *4'33"* (*Four Minutes Thirty-three Seconds*, 1952), a silent composition for piano consisting of whatever sounds happened to occur in the performance hall, Cage embraced a combination of the unpredictable, the real, and the mundane. His *Landscape No. 4* (1951) combined broadcasts of 12 radios tuned at random; *Variations IV,* at a Los Angeles art gallery in 1965, merged diverse media—records, tapes, radio broadcasts, billowing static—plus live chatter, traffic noise, and glasses tinkling at a bar set up for the concert. The "media bites" in *Variations IV* included grand opera, a crooner, news of war, a Beethoven symphony, and a woman complaining of desertion by her husband. Hence the typical Cage event (co-directed in the case of *Variations IV* by David Tudor) often combined not just different sorts of music in no particular order, but also miscellaneous sounds ordinarily considered non-musical. Owing to the large role played by chance, when the typical Cage event was re-staged, neither the sounds nor their order would likely be the same.

Subsequently, in *Variations V* at New York City's Lincoln Center, intersections of dancers and light beams activated electronic sounds. The dancers were members of Merce Cunningham's company, for which Cage served as music director. Collaborators since 1942, Cage and Cunningham shared several notions about making art. Both individuals sought to assemble wholes

out of parts (such as sounds and dancers' gestures) that originated and func-
tioned independently—or as independently as possible. Each part was considered to have value in itself equal to that of any other, with no part
subordinate to an overriding theme, structure, or story—or to the artist's ego
and emotion. Sound and choreography, often created separately, could remain
strangers up to the moment of performance. If the Cage/Cunningham strategy did not fully isolate every part of every work, and thereby eradicate all in-
timations of connection and wholeness, it surely loosened the usual bonds.
Further, in highlighting disjunctions among the parts, Cage in particular em-
phasized hybrid or collage-like aspects of the artwork.

Such hybrid interests contributed to the composer's life-long probing of
borders between art and non-art, music and non-music, and, as his collaboration with Cunningham indicates, between diverse art forms. He was inspired in his hybrid experiments by the work of earlier American composers
including Ives, Thomson, and the French-born Varèse. At the same time,
Cage's inclination to link and merge art forms, along with his belief in painting's avant-garde primacy, prompted him to compare musical precedents for
his work to breakthroughs in painting. In 1959, for instance, one year after
Rauschenberg's *Odalisk*, Cage likened Thomson's *Symphony on a Hymn Tune*
(1926–28), a hybrid of musical styles or approaches markedly less dissonant
than any by Cage, to a "painting that substitutes for brush and pigment scis-
sors, paste, and various ready-made materials."[38] Cage's artistic multi-tasking
also bore obvious affinities to mixed media "Happenings" staged by Allan
Kaprow and other artists starting in 1959, which combined music, dance,
painting, poetry readings, dramatic actions, dialogue, recordings, films, and
slides. Equally important was that Happenings probed the border between art
and life, and, much as Cage had done, celebrated energies of chance, humor,
anarchy, incongruity, fragmentation, and aggression. Indeed, a hybrid or
mixed-means event Cage initiated in 1952 at Black Mountain College in
North Carolina has been credited as the first Happening.[39]

When Robert Venturi asserted in *Complexity and Contradiction in Architecture* (1979) that he preferred "elements which are hybrid rather than 'pure,'"
and "messy vitality" to "obvious unity," he summoned yet another artistic dis-
cipline to the hybrid banner.[40] Further, Venturi suggested he did so in order to
keep faith with modern life: ". . . I speak of a complex and contradictory architecture based on the richness and ambiguity of modern experience," he

said, adding that only an architecture rooted in human reality could achieve both "vitality and validity."[41] Earlier twentieth-century architecture's emphasis on purity and rationality, he argued, failed to reflect, and often repressed, major tensions and uncertainties of modern life that had to be acknowledged if people were to achieve a measure of inner peace and relief. In support of his view, Venturi quoted August Heckscher: "A feeling for paradox allows seemingly dissimilar things to exist side by side, their very incongruity suggesting a kind of truth."[42]

Like Luis Buñuel, Venturi ascribed moral value to an artistic strategy, stressing that hybrid form's complexity, contradiction, and incongruity made it particularly vital and faithful to modern experience. Moral value has been attributed also to Cage's creations. Although some observers have considered the composer's work morally neutral or insouciant, others have found it distinctly affirmative—mirroring at once Zen Buddhism, democratic visions of equality and freedom, and anarchic and libertarian rejections of authority.

The implication that hybrid form has distinctive value because it rings particularly true to modern perception and experience reaches further, of course. In 1922 the hybrid generic and stylistic makeup of both James Joyce's *Ulysses* and T.S. Eliot's *The Waste Land*, for instance, could be taken to reflect not only the eclectic genius of each author, but also an increasingly urban and cosmopolitan world, the globe as a collage city—or, in Eliot's grim phrase, an "immense panorama of futility and anarchy"[43]—in which diverse peoples and styles interact, and human awareness and historical consciousness expand. In any case, as British novelist and critic Anthony Burgess has written, in *Ulysses*, a vast epic once reviled as pornography, "Each chapter . . . has a distinct style of its own . . . in the Maternity Hospital scene the prose imitates all the English literary styles from *Beowulf* to Carlyle and beyond. . . ."[44] Burgess has commented along similar lines that *The Waste Land* "quotes frequently from the literatures of Europe and India (in the original), uses a rapidly shifting point-of-view . . . and uses verse which owes something to practically every English poet of the past, though Eliot's voice is always heard clearly enough."[45]

Another oft-cited feature of hybrid form and stylistic diversity in both *Ulysses* and *The Waste Land*, though particularly in the former, concerns the merging of stream of consciousness and inner monologue with objective description of external events. Such fascination with cross-plays of inner and outer life, shared by other writers including Virginia Woolf and William Faulkner, seems consistent with the growing emphasis in the 1920s and '30s on multiple psychological dimensions of human experience as illumined by figures such as William James, Henri Bergson, Sigmund Freud, and Carl Jung. Visual collages by Max Ernst, including *UNE SEMAINE DE BONTÉ* (1933), a Surrealist novel in pictures, further reflect these psychological interests. As a student at a German university, Ernst explored Freud's work, which viewed human personality as a dynamic mingling of id, ego, and superego, of conscious and unconscious, and of rational pieties and primitive drives. Indeed, the highly complex, often self-contradictory existence described by Freud seemed to call for hybrid form in visual, musical, and literary art that aspired to be faithful to modern experience.

Perhaps like art and human personality, the physical world over the last century also has taken on increasingly hybrid dimensions, as it has come to appear less pure, simple, constant, and knowable than before.[46] Mass and energy, for instance, are no longer viewed as entirely fixed and separate, but as interconnected and transmutable. A similar situation pertains to space and time. Further, a photon of light is not purely a particle, nor a wave, but both, and much the same applies to the appearance and behavior of an electron. Recently, subatomic items like quarks, once regarded as particles, have been reconstrued as strings or strands of energy, oscillating in eleven dimensions or so, but tiny enough to be particle-like. When Venturi said he favored "messy vitality over obvious unity" and "both-and" over "either-or,"[47] his aesthetic and philosophical direction was in step with scientific description of the physical world. Further, his focus on contradiction nicely corresponded to scientific belief that the universe was very different from how it appeared. Things might look and feel solid, for instance, but consist nonetheless of atoms that are mostly empty space. "All that is solid melts into air," Karl Marx's well-known summation of nineteenth-century industrial capitalism and globalization, resonates in scientific accounts of physical facts a century later. To see, grasp, or define the physical world proves difficult, if not impossible, partly because things possess hybrid properties and often shift in appearance and behavior unpredictably. Especially in the case of the subatomic universe, moreover, entities seem to change with the very effort to pinpoint them. Physical reality emerges as not only complex and contradictory, but also, somewhat like a performance conceived by John Cage, indeterminate.

Hybrid Film in Hollywood

Venturi lamented that architecture lagged behind other art forms in espousing complexity and contradiction, and in achieving hybrid validity and vitality. However, one might argue that Hollywood cinema, an industrial enterprise requiring not only huge financial outlays and returns, but also, even more than does architecture, the approval of a mass audience, has been the greater laggard. The notion that life is scarcely pure and simple can be no less evident in Hollywood than elsewhere. Paul Haggis, author of the script for *Million Dollar Baby* and director of *Crash*, which won the Academy Award for Best Picture in 2006, has remarked, "There's no such thing as a pure act of any sort. . . . There's no pure act of hatred, no pure act of love. There's always some selfishness in an act of love, and in an act of hate there's probably always something that mitigates it. Maybe we all embody these contradictions."[48] But while characters in just about every Hollywood genre have manifested such contradictions, the contradictions have not yielded hybrid generic forms in Hollywood as radical as those in other traditions that have responded to modern life's distinctive complexity and indeterminacy. Among Hollywood genres or types of film, possibly *film noir* has been the most sensitive to modern circumstances, but without pursuing strongly hybrid directions. It would seem that Hollywood's conception of what the general public would pay for has inhibited such a course.

To be sure, hybrid expression exists in Hollywood cinema, but within limits, as the conventions fostering such expression simultaneously restrain it. "The Forgotten Man" number concluding *Gold Diggers of 1933* (Mervyn LeRoy and Busby Berkeley), for instance, mounts a statement of despair and defeat relating to World War I and the 1930s Depression far more graphic and severe than anything prior in the film. But this eruption of truth exists in the film merely as entertainment, a stage performance, a spasm of unreality, cordoned off from the film's offstage reality (and from the reality outside the film, so quickly does the screen turn black once the number ends—except for the white letters announcing the end). "The Forgotten Man" follows the happy culmination of the main characters' offstage quest to find romance and marriage in the Depression while composing, funding, and casting a Broadway musical. Although the melody and moral impetus for "The Forgotten Man" arise early in the story, little prepares the audience for the number's grim depiction of men taken from their land and their lovers, shipped off to war to be

wounded or killed—or to be abandoned, when they survive the war, to beg-
gary and humiliation during the Depression. Not only the sequence's theme
and narrative diverge from the rest of the film, but also its mise-en-scène. Suddenly soldiers trudge hopelessly through rain, darkness, thunder, and dirt,
while houses that are slanted, twisted, and crushed together at the start of the
number evoke German Expressionism. Offstage, the dialogue in the female
cast members' comfortable, quotidian apartment has cited the imminent danger of poverty and starvation, but no one has looked or acted much the worse
for it. Indeed, the characters' faces, chatter, and movements have been quick
and upbeat, though predictable, just as the weather has been fair. As indicated
above, however, the contrast posed by "The Forgotten Man" number prompts
only minimal puzzlement and disturbance in the movie's spectator because
convention confines the number to a zone of performance not to be merged
or confused with the rest of the film. Something similar may be said of the celebrated "Shadow Waltz" number earlier in the film, which, though more relevant thematically than "The Forgotten Man," presents a more radical shift of
mise-en-scène, as the human body and other solid matter recede into lush
blackness broken only by the floating neon outlines of violins.

    Less confined and controlled than the anomalies in *Gold Diggers of 1933* are
hybrid elements in the visually more staid and uniform *Forty-Second Street*
(1933, Lloyd Bacon and Busby Berkeley), a film earlier the same year in which
grief of one kind or another suppresses the energy and pleasure of casting,
funding, and rehearsing a Broadway musical. In particular, the manic anguish
of the show's ailing director (Warner Baxter) and the frustrations of its fading
star (Bebe Daniels) cast a pall that stifles even the film's climactic and oft-
quoted music-and-dance numbers. Further, as neither the director nor the
star seems distinctively vital or talented, the suffering of each registers as
maudlin more than heroic. The entire film, in fact, suggests a musical genre in
its nascent years swathed in dirge and melodrama.

    Possibly hybrid form has thrived better in Hollywood farce than in the mu-
sical, since farce along with satire and comedy tends more naturally to challenge order and authority. Rather than being segregated from the rest of the
story, for example, the explosion of space, noise, and unlikely action in the war
montage in *Duck Soup* (1933, Leo McCarey) seems integral. While the sequence differs audio-visually from other moments such as Harpo's silent attack, rendered in long takes, on a rival popcorn vendor's hat, the forbidden

pleasures of either committing or witnessing assaults on reason and propriety knit the two sequences together, like much else in the film. Indeed, a possible problem is that the film's anarchic stirrings eventually seem almost tame since they are incessant and predictable rather than exceptional. In addition, *Duck Soup*'s protected, studio-enclosed look signals that the mayhem will yield little if any real harm, and that comedy's promise of a happy ending will be kept. Moreover, the film's cinematic style, much less vibrant than would appear from the contrast I have observed between Harpo's long-take attack and the war montage—and less stimulating than Groucho's occasionally smart linguistic turns, lends almost wearisome constancy to the whole.

While unfettered hybrid form remains unusual in Hollywood to the present day, such form has recently appeared more frequently than before—in gangster films, war films, comedies, family melodramas, documentaries, and other types of film. In this recent elaboration of hybrid cinema, the distribution if not the production of which has generally been financed by Hollywood, diverse generic and stylistic currents intersect in ways more glaring and anarchic than in the past. *Hollywood Hybrids: Mixing Genres in Contemporary Films* examines in five chapters this phenomenon of magnified, emboldened hybrid form.

THE ORGANIZATION OF *HOLLYWOOD HYBRIDS*

The first chapter, "Fact and Fiction," centers on documentaries, including films by Errol Morris, who made not only *The Fog of War* (2003), winner of the Academy Award for Best Documentary, but also films more emphatically hybrid in form such as *Mr. Death: The Rise and Fall of Fred A. Leuchter, Jr.* (1999), *Fast, Cheap and Out of Control* (1997), and *The Thin Blue Line* (1989). *Bowling for Columbine* (2002, Michael Moore), *Fahrenheit 9/11* (2004, Michael Moore), *Bright Leaves* (2003, Ross McElwee), *Tarnation* (2004, Jonathan Caouette), and *Capturing the Friedmans* (2003, Andrew Jarecki) also figure in this chapter, along with *The Truman Show* (1998, Peter Weir) and *Best in Show* (1999, Christopher Guest), two comic fictional meditations about reality television and documentary film. In the works discussed in this chapter, diverse generic and stylistic impulses converge in investigations of truth and reality, which remain elusive partly owing to human fear, myopia, greed, and dishonesty. Further obfuscating truth and reality in these films is modern media's preoccupation with entertainment, celebrity, and economic and political gain.

Indeed, media "coverage" in these films often means not the discovery and communication of truth, but its concealment.

"Gangster and Warrior," chapter two, focuses on *Fargo* (1996, Ethan and Joel Coen), *Pulp Fiction* (1994, Quentin Tarantino), and *Three Kings* (1999, David O. Russell)—films that allude primarily to film noir, the gangster film, and the war film, while incorporating aspects of farce, comedy, melodrama, horror, and tragedy. Further, somewhat like the documentaries highlighted in the first chapter, the fiction films discussed here probe the divide between fact and fiction. They also bear on Salman Rushdie's hint that hybrid form's "new and unexpected combinations" of generic and stylistic modes reflect and engender more vibrant human consciousness. In particular, *Fargo*, *Pulp Fiction*, and *Three Kings* feature characters who are confronted with "new and unexpected" perspectives of thought and feeling. In *Pulp Fiction* and *Three Kings*, these characters react by sharing—or entering into—such unfamiliar perspectives; and as they do so, their humanness expands and grows more generous. Hybrid cinema consequently emerges as a vehicle for exploring hybrid dimensions of human identity.

Chapter three, "Melodrama and Teen Romance," centers on *Blue Velvet* (1986, David Lynch), *Far from Heaven* (2002, Todd Haynes), and *Poison* (1991, Haynes), as well as on *All that Heaven Allows* (1956, Douglas Sirk), the classic melodrama cited throughout *Far from Heaven*. Like the works discussed in "Gangster and Warrior," these films combine diverse generic and stylistic modes while exploring hybrid aspects of human experience. In *Far from Heaven*, characters ponder the wisdom of "mixing with other worlds" socially and economically; in *Blue Velvet* and *Poison*, they observe or are immersed in convergences of fantasy, dream, and reality. But the shifting currents of hybrid cinema and hybrid experience in this chapter take a darker turn than in "Gangster and Warrior." In "Melodrama and Teen Romance," hybrid form renders torments of male and female desire and of family life and teenage aspiration. In the films discussed in this chapter, the nuclear family is fractured or dissolved. Community becomes tenuous. Virtue gives way to perversity and violence. What survives of moral order appears weak and suspect.

Comedy and tragedy intersect repeatedly in hybrid cinema, recasting and redirecting one another. Some of the most powerful and sustained tragicomic conjunctions in film history occur prior to recent hybrid cinema, however—in Charlie Chaplin's films, for example, including *The Gold Rush* (1925), *Modern*

Times (1936), *The Great Dictator* (1940), and *Monsieur Verdoux* (1947). Such conjunctions appear also in the French-made *Rules of the Game* (1939, Jean Renoir), as well as in *Dr. Strangelove. Or How I Learned to Stop Worrying and Love the Bomb* (1964, Stanley Kubrick) and in *Nashville* (1975, Robert Altman). Although, aside from *Verdoux*, Chaplin's films are usually termed comedies, they address terrors of starvation, economic depression, global war, Nazism, and genocide. They also confront the dehumanizing costs of industrialization and the contrast between humankind's technological progress and its sociopolitical failures. The obvious hazards of technological power in the hands of sociopolitical immaturity are central also in *Dr. Strangelove*'s depiction of humankind's descent into nuclear war.

Recent hybrid films in Hollywood such as *Slacker* (1991, Richard Linklater) *Pulp Fiction*, and *Broken Flowers* (2005, Jim Jarmusch) are perhaps less explicitly grounded than Chaplin's films and *Dr. Strangelove* in dilemmas that make newspaper headlines around the globe. But such recent films are alert nonetheless to spiraling absurdity and contradiction in human experience today. In particular, they underscore the role of chance, irrationality, and accident, as opposed to that of logic and order, in contemporary convergences of tragedy and comedy. Hence these recent films take up an interest in chance and randomness that has been significant in all of the arts of the last century, as well as in diverse currents of international cinema such as Surrealism, Italian Neorealism, and the cinema of mental life advanced by Alain Resnais and Alain Robbe-Grillet. Titled "Tragicomic Accidents," chapter four considers the interplay of accident, tragedy, and comedy in classic works by Renoir, Chaplin, Kubrick, and Altman, as well as in recent hybrid films like *Slacker*, *Pulp Fiction*, and *Broken Flowers*.

As I have indicated, antecedents of recent hybrid cinema in Hollywood include not only films made in the United States and around the world, but also works of art in other mediums such as music, dance, painting, poetry, the novel, and architecture. Indeed, hybrid form has become almost commonplace in artistic and cultural enterprise during the past hundred years. No surprise, then, that it figures prominently in contemporary foreign films that have been widely acclaimed. Chapter five, "Global Parallels," addresses hybrid cinema as a global phenomenon, focusing on recent examples from China, Germany, Hong Kong, and Spain. The films include *The World* (2004, Jia Zhang-ke); *Run Lola Run* (1998, Tom Tykwer); *Shaolin Soccer* (2001, Stephen Chow); and *Talk to Her* (2002, Pedro Almodóvar).

NOTES

1. For an amplication of this view, see Daniel Mendelsohn, "It's Only a Movie," *New York Review of Books*, Vol. L, No. 20, December 18, 2003, pp. 38–41.

2. See John Pavlus's discussion of the cinematography in *Kill Bill*, in "A Bride Vows Vengeance," *American Cinematographer*, Vol. 84, No. 10, October 2003, pp. 33-47.

3. Pavlus, "A Bride Vows Vengeance," p. 37.

4. Pavlus, "A Bride Vows Vengeance," p. 36.

5. Larissa MacFarquhar, "The Movie Lover," *New Yorker*, October 20, 2003, p. 155.

6. Stuart Klawans underscores the familial aspects of *Kill Bill* in his review, "The Avengers," in *The Nation*, November 10, 2003, pp. 33–34.

7. Quoted in MacFarquhar, "The Movie Lover," p. 157.

8. Quoted in Manohla Dargis, "Quentin Tarantino on *Pulp Fiction*," in Jim Hillier (ed.), *American Independent Cinema* (London: British Film Institute, 2001), p. 242.

9. Dargis, "Quentin Tarantino on *Pulp Fiction*," p. 243.

10. Dargis, "Quentin Tarantino on *Pulp Fiction*," p. 244.

11. Quoted in Kwame Anthony Appiah, "Toward a New Cosmopolitanism," *New York Times Magazine*, January 1, 2006, Section 6, p. 52.

12. Manny Farber, *Movies* (New York: Hillstone, 1971), p. 8.

13. Sergei Eisenstein, "A Dialectic Approach to Film Form," in *Film Form and Film Sense*, ed. and trans. Jay Leyda (Cleveland: Meridian, 1964), p. 58.

14. Dziga Vertov, *KINO-EYE. The Writings of Dziga Vertov*, trans. Kevin O'Brien, ed. Annette Michelson (Berkeley: University of California Press, 1984), p. 18.

15. Vertov, *KINO-EYE*, p. 17.

16. Quoted in Jay Leyda, *KINO. A History of the Russian and Soviet Film* (New York: Macmillan, 1960), p. 244.

17. Luis Buñuel, *My Last Sigh*, trans. Abigail Israel (New York: Vintage, 1984), p. 103.

18. Buñuel, *My Last Sigh*, p. 104.

19. Buñuel, *My Last Sigh*, p. 109.

20. Sitney was quoted in A. O. Scott's obituary, "Stan Brakhage, Avant-Garde Filmmaker, Dies at 70," *New York Times*, March 12, 2003.

21. More precisely, Godard said of *Breathless*, "Although I felt ashamed of it at one time, I do like *À Bout de Souffle* very much, but now I see where it belongs—along with *Alice in Wonderland*. I thought it was *Scarface*." See *Godard on Godard*, translation and commentary by Tom Milne (New York: Viking, 1972), p. 175.

22. Godard, *Godard on Godard*, p. 40.

23. Godard, *Godard on Godard*, p. 239.

24. Godard, *Godard on Godard*, p. 239.

25. Godard, *Godard on Godard*, p. 239.

26. Godard, *Godard on Godard*, p. 9.

27. Jean-Luc Godard, *Weekend/Wind from the East* (New York: Simon and Schuster, 1972), p. 56. The dialogue for *Weekend* was translated by Marianne Sinclair.

28. Godard, *Weekend/Wind from the East*, p. 50.

29. Godard, *Godard on Godard*, p. 239.

30. Godard, *Godard on Godard*, p. 173.

31. Godard, *Godard on Godard*, p. 173.

32. Godard, *Weekend/Wind from the East*, p. 24.

33. Godard, *Weekend/Wind from the East*, p. 51.

34. Quoted in Annette Michelson's introduction to Nagisa Oshima, *Cinema, Censorship, and the State: The Writings of Nagisa Oshima, 1956–1978* (Cambridge, MA: MIT Press, 1992), p. 5.

35. Tomás Gutiérrez Alea and Edmundo Desnoes, *Memories of Underdevelopment and Inconsolable Memories* (New Brunswick, NJ: Rutgers University Press, 1990), p. 57.

36. Quoted in Calvin Tomkins, *Off the Wall. Robert Rauschenberg and the Art World of Our Time* (New York: Penguin, 1985), p. 134.

37. This statement by *Time*'s art critic Robert Hughes is quoted in Calvin Tomkins, "Rauschenberg," *New Yorker*, May 23, 2005, p. 76.

38. Quoted in Carol J. Oja, "The USA, 1918–45," in Robert P. Morgan (ed.), *Music Society and Modern Times: From World War I to the Present* (Englewood Cliffs, NJ: Prentice Hall, 1994), p. 211.

39. See Richard Kostelanetz, *John Cage (ex)plain(ed)* (New York: Schirmer, 1996), p. 94.

40. Robert Venturi, *Complexity and Contradiction in Architecture* (New York: Museum of Modern Art, 1979), p. 16.

41. Venturi, *Complexity and Contradiction in Architecture*, p. 16.

42. Venturi, *Complexity and Contradiction in Architecture*, p. 16. Culturally and politically influential, Heckscher served as editorial writer for the *Herald Tribune*, chairman of the International Council of the Museum of Modern Art, member of the Council on Foreign Relations, and head of Parks, Recreation and Cultural Affairs for New York City.

43. Quoted in F.O. Matthiessen, *The Achievement of T.S. Eliot. An Essay on the Nature of Poetry* (New York: Oxford University Press, 1959), p. 40.

44. Anthony Burgess, *English Literature. A Survey for Students* (London: Longman, 1974), p. 218.

45. Burgess, *English Literature*, p. 217.

46. See, for example, Bill Bryson, *A Short History of Nearly Everything* (New York: Broadway Books, 2003), especially "A New Age Dawns," pp. 113–187.

47. Venturi, *Complexity and Contradiction in Architecture*, p. 16.

48. Quoted in David M. Halbfinger, "Filmmaker Finds Métier Exploring a Gray Zone," *New York Times*, March 14, 2005, p. B7.

1

Fact and Fiction

Since its birth as a commercial medium in the 1890s, cinema has rendered fact as well as fiction to audiences around the globe. In France, the first Lumière films, including travelogues called *documentaires*, focused on actual life; soon after, Georges Méliès, parading the camera's knack for magical effects, created fantastic fictions. Thomas Edison's studio in the United States turned out both fact and fiction. Then, as movies grew in duration from one minute or less to 90 minutes or more, narrative fiction became dominant, as it has remained since 1918. Yet cinematic fact and fiction have rarely been divorced, if only because sounds and images of the actual world "imprint" both kinds of cinema. Moreover, fiction addresses the emotions and thoughts of actual human existence, while films of fact, persistently framing, re-arranging, and interpreting life, assume prerogatives ascribed to fiction. If nothing else, films of fact—or "documentaries," as John Grierson preferred to call them—entail what he termed "a creative treatment of actuality."[1]

BLURRED BORDERS IN DOCUMENTARY FILMS

That documentary, like fiction film, inevitably conjoins fact and fiction is but one reason to include it in an exploration of hybrid cinema. Another is that U.S. documentaries at the start of the twenty-first century, as in the closing decades of the twentieth, have focused on the hazy divide between fact and fiction with increasing explicitness and frequency. *Nanook of the North* (1922,

Robert Flaherty), often considered the first mature documentary, depicted Nanook and his family dressing and hunting in the manner of earlier generations, but not their own, and sleeping in a structure that was just half an igloo built specifically for the filming. Such deception might disturb the innocence of some spectators and buttress the cynicism of others. Flaherty's view was that his goal of capturing the essence of Eskimo identity justified the fakery. In any case, *Nanook* itself does not explicitly acknowledge or address questions it provokes as to borders between fact and fiction—or, for that matter, between fact and truth. On the other hand, such questions are front and center, though not necessarily resolved, in recent documentaries like *The Thin Blue Line*, *Bright Leaves*, *Bowling for Columbine*, *Fahrenheit 9/11*, and *The Fog of War*. Yet a further reason to explore documentary in relation to hybrid cinema is that the former has become a powerful magnet for diverse excerpts from fiction films, news footage, commercials, cartoons, and government and corporate infomercials. Far more than *Nanook* and other documentaries prior to the 1970s, recent documentaries constitute arrays of generic and stylistic signals. Among examples of "magnetic" or hybrid documentaries, in addition to films cited above as probing borders between fact and fiction, are *Tarnation*, *The Atomic Café* (1982, Kevin Rafferty, Jayne Loader, Pierce Rafferty), and *Hearts and Minds* (1975, Peter Davis), the last a winner, like *Bowling for Columbine* and *The Fog of War*, of the Oscar for best feature documentary. Also notable is that the success of documentaries at the U.S. box office has grown in tandem with their tendency to explore relations between fact and fiction and to incorporate excerpts from generically diverse films.

Fiction as Documentary

As plainly as any recent documentary, *Bright Leaves* imports film excerpts and links up fact and fiction. Ross McElwee, who in 1986 completed the celebrated autobiographical documentary *Sherman's March*, heads south again in *Bright Leaves* to reconsider his roots. In North Carolina where he was born, he visits his cousin John McElwee, a collector of 16mm and 35mm prints of old movies; John introduces him to *Bright Leaf* (1950, Michael Curtiz), a Hollywood melodrama about a nineteenth-century tobacco grower, starring Gary Cooper, Patricia Neal, and Lauren Bacall. While Ross's documentary incorporates excerpts from additional sources, including home movies of his son and father, *Bright Leaf* provokes in him particular wonder about the film medium.

For he finds himself regarding this fiction film as a documentary about his great grandfather, cheated of a potential fortune by a villainous competitor who in actual life founded the Duke tobacco empire; if not for ill deeds dramatized in *Bright Leaf*, opines Ross, Duke University today would be McElwee University. The widow of the author of the novel that inspired *Bright Leaf*, however, denies that the book was based on Ross's great grandfather's life, or on the life of any other actual person that her husband knew or had in mind. But Ross continues to marvel that he has found documentary content in a Hollywood melodrama, and that, most likely, more than one documentary resides in every fiction film. To advance this point, he replays what he considers an unscripted gesture of longing and indecision by Patricia Neal as she kisses Gary Cooper in *Bright Leaf*. Since Ross holds that her gesture reveals something of the intense but troubled off-screen romance at the time between Neal and Cooper, more than it does any experience of the characters they portray, he asks voice-over, "Does this not constitute a kind of documentary moment, a sort of home movie?" He even visits Neal to firm up his sense of her former off-screen relationship with Cooper.

Somewhat like McElwee in *Bright Leaves*, Michael Moore embeds portions of fiction films in *Bowling for Columbine* and endows them with documentary meaning and value. Put another way, he uses editing, voice-over narration, and other devices to expose fictional excerpts as documentaries in disguise. An early example in *Columbine* is the heroic image from a Hollywood fiction of Charlton Heston gustily firing an automatic weapon at an antagonist in black cloak and hood, who promptly leaps from a terrace to his doom. Before and after the fictive image of Heston, he and Moore appear in separate candid shots aiming rifles, while Moore's voice-over explains that they both grew up in gun-friendly Michigan and joined the National Rifle Association. However, no image of Moore in this film matches the zest for killing, as though it were a form of play, exhibited in Moore's insert of the Hollywood Heston, who, off-screen, serves as the NRA's zealous president. Further, that Heston's mortal target in the fiction seems devoid of moral awareness and humanity perhaps makes it less surprising that Heston, or at least the zestful killer he portrays, seems utterly fatuous.

The question arises, consequently, whether an actor or spectator identifying with Heston's movie persona could learn thereby to take killing and dying seriously. Or is it just such imagery that inhibits sober and realistic reckonings, and that accounts in part for the extraordinary number of Americans slain by guns each year? Might Heston's blithe and fictive warrior, then, constitute a documentary moment or home movie of popular consciousness in the USA— and of what historian Daniel Boorstin once called "the thicket of unreality" Americans cultivate between themselves and "the facts of life" by their use of modern media?[2] The playwright Arthur Miller, referring to President Ronald Reagan's purported "inability to distinguish movies he had seen from actual events in which he had participated,"[3] voiced a concern similar to Boorstin's. Noting the ubiquity of role-playing, not just in the movies but in the vast, me-dia-saturated universe outside the cinema, Miller added, ". . . when one is sur-rounded by such a roiling mass of consciously contrived performances it gets harder and harder for a lot of people to locate reality anymore."[4]

In *Bowling for Columbine* and *Fahrenheit 9/11*, each of which set box-office records for documentaries exhibited in commercial theatres, Moore as the central character engages a reality blanketed by the images and sounds of mul-tiple genres and styles. Comedy, horror, westerns, melodrama, cartoons, doc-umentary, TV news, interviews, commercials and infomercials—all flood the scene he enters. But in the manner of Heston's movie warrior, the abundant images and sounds represent to Moore a thicket of unreality, rather than truth, and yield surprisingly scant diversity of experience. In both of his doc-umentaries, Moore quotes from various genres of mainstream film and tele-vision, including chilling TV newscasts, to argue that these media uniformly provoke fear and aggression against mistaken objects, and ultimately promote political, economic, and military oppression of most Americans by a hypo-critical elite.

However, Moore does not merely relate problems such as war, poverty, and pollution, as well as neglect and murder of one's fellow citizens, to a media-cultivated thicket of unreality. He also strives to highlight and create alterna-tive media signifiers that are truer to reality as he sees it. Somewhat in the spirit of Mikhail Bakhtin's cultural theories, he seeks to replace the relatively univocal authority of popular media with a broader, more constructive dia-logue. While it can be argued that Moore simply promotes a liberal bias as narrow as the ideology underlying the images and sounds he contests, at best this NRA card-carrier's documentaries inject into the false pluralism of to-day's media fresh ingredients more genuinely reflective of diverse worlds, more sensitive to the "immense plurality of experience."[5] In pursuit of such goals, Moore participates in his documentaries not simply as the main character on screen as well as the omnipresent voice-over narrator, but also as the resourceful editor who inserts archival footage unfamiliar to most spectators, and as the irreverent creator who stages subversive actions before his documentary camera, turning his critical imagination into reality.

Early in *Fahrenheit 9/11*, after Moore, voice-over, asks whether the reversal of the 2000 Presidential election—with first Al Gore and then George Bush declared the winner—was a dream, he presents scenes unfamiliar to most viewers of his documentary. These moments include African American representatives in Congress challenging the integrity of the vote, and Gore, who chairs the meeting as vice president, dutifully rejecting their petition since not one senator has agreed to sign it. Other footage reveals angry crowds, out of frame in most mainstream coverage of Bush's 2000 inauguration, protesting his victory as he passes in his inaugural limousine. Soon the film also features an unidentified boy being tucked into a sumptuous bed after Moore voice-over describes Bush, apparently relaxed after a lengthy vacation at his Texas ranch, visiting Florida and its governor (his brother), and getting yet more rest "that night in a bed made with fine French linens." Then, inter-cut with credits for Moore's film, Bush and key members of his administration appear, presumably off-camera, as they are made up for TV. Among them, a smiling Paul Wolfowitz, Deputy Secretary of Defense and a chief architect of Bush's Iraq policy, readies his comb with his spittle. More somber footage shows President Bush, in a schoolroom as children read "My Pet Goat," sitting immobilized for seven minutes after news of the second attack on the World Trade Center has been whispered in his ear. Moore not only tells the spectator how long Bush remained impassive in his chair, but also acts as the President's inner voice, wondering aloud who double-crossed him by mounting the WTC attacks.

In addition to nonfiction footage, Moore deploys fiction to criticize Bush's leadership and worldview. A scene from the TV detective drama *Dragnet* is quoted to argue that Bin Laden family members should not have been allowed to leave the United States after 9/11 without first being interrogated by FBI and other investigators. Later, the faces of Bush, British Prime Minister Tony Blair, Vice President Dick Cheney, and other officials are affixed to the equestrian bodies of *Bonanza*'s stars to underscore what has been termed Bush's *cowboyism* in launching the 2003 Iraq invasion. Snippets from other Westerns, whose characters vow to "smoke out" the enemy, support the claim that Bush's lingo, like his outlook, derive from lowbrow fiction. Citing the "coalition of the willing" that joined the invasion of Iraq, Moore lays out a fictive montage that incorporates hapless Vikings from Iceland, Max Schreck's vampire in *Nosferatu* (1922) representing Romania, and a fleet of scurrying monkeys sent by Morocco to detonate Iraqi landmines. Finally, embattled U.S. soldiers in Iraq are shown gathering energy and courage by playing the Bloodhound Gang's "The Roof is on Fire," with its hortatory refrain, "Burn, motherfucker, burn."

Documentary as Invention and Exposé

As suggested earlier, Moore not only recasts and deconstructs prevailing media images and sounds, but also provides ones of his own devising. In *Documentary: A History of the Non-Fiction Film*, Erik Barnouw remarks that "true documentarists . . . serve as catalysts, not as inventors. Unlike the fiction artist, they are dedicated to not inventing." But rather than restrict himself to "selecting and arranging . . . findings"[6] in the manner of Barnouw's model, Moore interjects his own images, sounds, words, and deeds, thereby redefining and reinventing the world he discovers. While this invasive drive is nowhere more evident than in *Bowling for Columbine*, the Academy Award winner, it also appears in *Fahrenheit 9/11*—not just in instances I have discussed above, but in others as well, as Moore himself stages and enacts events. Informed, for example, that legislators frequently do not read the legislation they vote on, Moore in an ice cream truck advances toward the nation's Capitol reciting the Patriot Act through a loudspeaker. Shifting his focus later in the film to the disproportionate burden of war borne by the poor, he enjoins members of Congress sauntering past him near the Capitol to tell their children to enlist in the armed services (where, at the time, just one was serving).

Bowling for Columbine

Moore's interventions, as I have indicated, are yet more radical, or at least more protracted and numerous, in *Bowling for Columbine*. Early on he inserts home movies that show him as a child with his first toy gun, succeeded by images of him as an adult wielding an actual rifle. The latter are inter-cut with comparable documentary and fictional shots of the adult Heston with a rifle. The Oscar-winning actor turned NRA president embodies from the outset at-

In Bowling for Columbine *and other Michael Moore documentaries, Moore becomes an active participant and even creates dramatic events, as in this scene at K-Mart, a retail store that sells bullets along with more common household goods. Alliance Atlantis/Dog Eat Dog/United Broadcasting/The Kobal Collection.*

titudes targeted by Moore, much as Bush does in *Fahrenheit 9/11*. Prior to these rifle displays in *Bowling for Columbine*, however, Moore films a scene specifically for his documentary in which he opens an account at a bank that awards rifles to new patrons. (He fills out the account application snappily, pausing mainly over whether he has ever been "adjudicated mentally defective.") Further, his meditation on the April 20, 1999, Columbine High School massacre leads him, along with two of 24 students wounded in the shootings, which also left a teacher and 12 students dead, to create a drama at K-Mart. Moore's two collaborators, one of whom was paralyzed in the attack, seek to return bullets purchased at a K-Mart store that remain lodged in their bodies. The sequence expands until Moore and his cohorts, having gained wide media attention, persuade K-Mart to stop selling handgun ammunition. Thus a chain of incidents devised for the documentary by Moore and the stricken Columbine students alters what documentary scholar Bill Nichols might term "our shared historical world."[7]

Moore also stars in a short comic film, *Corporate Cops*, a pilot he creates to replace an actual TV series simply named *Cops*. While policemen in *Cops* focus on violent African American criminals, Moore's cinematic riposte features him in a "Corporate Crime Unit" jacket with a donut stuffed in his mouth, leaving his hands free to frisk and handcuff a white corporate executive emerging from a limousine whom Moore charges with exploiting the poor. Further, in *A Brief History of America*, an animated segment scripted by Moore for his documentary, he argues that various American communities—Pilgrims, slave owners, Western settlers, civil rights opponents in the 1950s and '60s—have coveted guns out of desperate fear and sloth. Thus Moore adds to the claim he makes in *Fahrenheit 9/11* as well as in *Bowling for Columbine* that America has become "the culture of fear."[8]

A climactic bit of staging occurs toward the end of *Bowling for Columbine* when Moore, as though a mere slovenly tourist, squats on an LA street corner perusing a map featuring the residences of Hollywood stars. Abetted by the magic of film editing, he next stands at the gate to Charlton Heston's Beverly Hills estate, where over the intercom he requests a meeting. Possibly in recognition of Moore's own star status, Heston agrees to see him the next morning. By this point, the film has investigated another tragedy: in what the film describes as "the youngest school shooting ever in U.S. history," at Buell Public School in Moore's hometown of Flint, Michigan, a six-year-old male first-grader, an African American, has shot and killed a female classmate, who is white. Moore's documentary has explained that the boy was sent by his welfare-to-work mother to stay with his uncle (in whose home he found the gun), when she could no longer pay the rent and had to travel and work all day and much of each night in a wealthy suburb miles away. Moore observes in his conversation with Heston that the actor was quick to lead an NRA rally in Flint shortly after the Buell killing, just as he had summoned the NRA faithful to a Colorado site near Columbine following that tragedy. Heston makes no apology. Another tense instant occurs as Heston answers Moore's query about the causes of U.S. gun violence by tentatively citing ethnic and civil rights problems. Perhaps the most dramatic moment, however, arises after Heston uncomfortably terminates the conversation, leaves the glass-walled space of the meeting, and ascends the path outside. Moore starts after him, stops, and holds up a large photograph of the girl slain at Buell. He implores Heston to turn around to face the photograph; when Heston refuses, Moore stands the image of the girl at the base of a pillar for anyone who takes the path to see, and only then departs.

It seems appropriate that the divide between these two NRA members reared in Michigan culminates in a dispute over confronting a visual image. Both men have made their careers in movies, and both have experienced the contemporary world's visual orientation, its absorption in media images even more than in words. Further, Moore has made it his filmmaking mission to upend what he considers to be popular media's thicket of unreality and culture of fear by advancing new and unfamiliar images as well as fresh takes on familiar ones. The wily homeliness of his own image or persona as he engages in this mission also seems relevant. Paunchy, unkempt, and slow-footed, he represents resistance by the ordinary citizen to falsity and unreality propagated by slick, mainstream media.

Under the headline, "The Man Behind the Secretary of State's Rock Star Image," *The New York Times* of December 5, 2005, reported that Condoleezza Rice's staff was "constantly looking out for image-making opportunities" since, explained a senior aide to Dr. Rice, "it is very important that she connects with the ordinary citizens of the countries she visits." The *Times* described one image-making success as follows: "As she landed in Tokyo early this year, waiting for her at the bottom of the stairs was Konishiki, the popular, 600-pound, Japanese-American sumo champion, decked out in a billowing black silk kimono." The next day, said a senior Japanese official quoted in the *Times*, Rice and Konishiki were "all over the newspapers."[9] Image-makers have staged opportunities also for President George W. Bush, of course, as in his landing on the USS *Abraham Lincoln* in the co-pilot's seat of a Navy S-3B to declare the end of major U.S. combat operations in Iraq under the huge banner, "Mission Accomplished." Another image memorialized the President holding a fake turkey on a quick Thanksgiving visit to U.S. soldiers in Iraq. With assists from cable news and other media, the Pentagon has proved equally creative, as in its Rambo-inflected accounts of Private Jessica Lynch's ordeal in Iraq and her rescue by U.S. Army Rangers and Navy Seals. Further, U.S. government agencies have distributed video promotions disguised as news to television stations throughout the country.

The immense influence of images devised at the highest levels of American politics, diplomacy, and entertainment has required that Moore *create* images, not just select and arrange them (as Barnouw described), so as to mount a full-scale challenge, which has constituted the primary subtext of his films. Evidence of his progress in this challenge extends beyond the Academy Award for *Bowling for Columbine* and acclaim for his documentaries at Cannes and other film festivals. In November 2005, White House Press Secretary Scott McClellan responded on CNN to Congressman John P. Murtha's proposal that U.S. troops withdraw from Iraq by accusing the 73-year-old former marine hero of "choosing the path of Michael Moore."[10] His biting tribute to Moore echoed official White House criticism of Murtha for "endorsing the policy positions of Michael Moore and the extreme liberal wings of the Democratic Party."[11]

Atomic Café

A blizzard of multi-generic images and sounds more relentless than in Moore's films pervades *The Atomic Café*, an earlier documentary about fear and violence in American society, relating specifically to America's development of atomic and hydrogen weapons. *The Atomic Café*'s cascade of film, radio, and television excerpts proceeds uninterrupted by a figure such as Moore—a visible narrator, critic, and creator residing outside the excerpts. Moreover, the inadvertent self-parody within some of these fragments requires no external embellishment. In one excerpt, the voices of two men possibly aloft in an attack bomber describe aerial film footage of the atomic destruction of Hiroshima and its people at the end of World War II: "It was a shambles," states one voice over the devastation. "Like Ebbets Field after a double header with the Giants," adds the second voice. Absurd similes posed by unseen as well as visible characters throughout this film account in part for its incongruous mix of farce, tragedy, and horror. And, were the film to include a guide or narrator external to this particular fragment, wherein Hiroshima is likened to a baseball diamond, and nuclear war to America's national pastime, the effect might simply be to mitigate and desecrate the shock.

In the absence of a critical narrator outside the fray, relatively sensible voices emerge within a few excerpts to warn of the growing madness. President Dwight D. Eisenhower, for instance, states that "advances of science have outraced our social consciousness," that humankind has progressed scientifically more than it is "capable of handling emotionally and intellectually." In another fragment, Seymour Melman, a professor of economics who co-chaired SANE (Committee for a Sane Nuclear Policy), warns that despite optimistic predictions such as those implicit in a 1950s cartoon that is cross-cut with his TV appearance in *The Atomic Café*, fallout shelters were unlikely to save Americans caught in the vicinity of an all-out nuclear strike. Like Eisenhower's warning, however, Melman's gets lost in the din of nuclear romance and sport—as someone sings, for instance, "my atomic love for you" over the image of a female fashion model posing before a phallic rocket.

Casting nuclear weaponry as a novel form of sport and romance reflects the desire of most people in *The Atomic Café* to domesticate the nuclear threat; they glamorize it, but also seek to make it familiar, homey, and controllable. Thus the film documents wide popular interest in atomic attire and food, and in building and outfitting family fallout shelters, which, to ensure the clan's survival and safety, will be closed to strangers in the event of an attack. The affinity suggested between nuclear weaponry and more familiar, less hazardous aspects of daily life reflects a nation's flight from reality; incongruous references to sport, romance, and domestic normality supplant fact with fiction. Put a bit differently, truth yields to "truthiness," a term proposed by Comedy Central's fake TV news pundit Stephen Colbert to designate "what you want to be true, as opposed to what the facts support."[12]

"HUMAN KIND CANNOT BEAR VERY MUCH REALITY"

The stampede toward fiction traced in *The Atomic Café*, somewhat like the fierce, wordless montages created by experimental filmmaker Bruce Conner, ultimately feels too profound and primal to be explained solely as a manifestation of media-generated unreality. Perhaps equally relevant to its nature and origin is the blunt observation in T.S. Eliot's *Burnt Norton* that ". . . human kind/ Cannot bear very much reality."[13] This claim haunts the shifting divide between fact and fiction not solely in recent documentaries, but also in fiction films, and in publications dealing with Americans' tolerance for reality.

The Truman Show

One instance in the fiction-film category is *The Truman Show* (1998, Peter Weir), starring Jim Carrey as insurance salesman Truman Burbank and Ed Harris as Christof, the God-like producer and creator of the long-running hit TV series, "The Truman Burbank Show." Since Truman's birth thirty years earlier, this documentary soap opera has deployed five thousand hidden cameras to chronicle his life in the fake island community of Seaheaven. The only world he has ever known, Seaheaven is an immense theatrical set (actually, Seaside, Florida—a planned, Disney-like town), entirely inhabited, except for the hero, by Christof's actors. Even Truman's wife is a cast member, deceiving Truman while plugging products to build the show's vast advertising revenues. When at last he discovers the sham that has enveloped him and asks, "Was nothing real?", Christof replies, "*You* were real"; when Truman then condemns him for making him live a lie, Christof responds, "There's no more truth out there than in the world I created for you." Despite this warning of "no more truth out there," whether because of the media, excessive role-playing, or humankind's inability to bear reality, Truman, who was "TV's first on-air conception" and the "first child legally adopted by a corporation," decides to escape Seaheaven and seek the truth for himself.

Somewhat like mock pundit Stephen Colbert, *The Fog of War: Eleven Lessons from the Life of Robert S. McNamara* stresses that the desires and predispositions underlying a quest such as Truman's can influence its outcome. McNamara, who served as Secretary of Defense during the Vietnam War, says he took as fact a report that North Vietnamese torpedoes targeted a U.S. naval destroyer, and consequently the United States bombed the enemy's homeland. Later, he explains, the United States learned that "freak weather effects" and "overeager sonar" had yielded the false impression of torpedoes. Perhaps, too, U.S. leaders had been "overeager." Hence McNamara draws a lesson about human nature: "We see incorrectly, or we see only half the story. . . . We were wrong, but we had . . . a mindset that led to that action." Interviewing McNamara from off-screen, filmmaker Errol Morris adds, "We see what we want to believe," to which McNamara assents. Toward film's end, the former Secretary of Defense revisits the complexity of knowing, as he paraphrases a closing passage in Eliot's *Burnt Norton* as follows: "We shall not cease from exploring, and at the end of our exploration we will return to where we started, and know the place for the first time."

As we can see, then, tensions regarding boundaries between fact and fiction in recent documentary and fiction films have coincided with heightened public dialogue about humankind's ability to "bear very much reality." Judge Richard Posner asserts in "Bad News," for instance, an essay about modern news media and the consumer, that the public does not want "uncomfortable truths."[14] A prolific author, U.S. Seventh Circuit Court of Appeals judge, and senior lecturer at University of Chicago Law School, Posner served as general counsel for the President's Task Force on Communications Policy during the Vietnam War. He contends that consumers of news media are neither civic-minded nor very interested in truth of any sort. Preferring entertainment to information—and perhaps enjoying the spectacle of competition above all—

the public seeks "factual accuracy" not for the sake of truth but "out of delight in unmasking the opposition's errors."[15]

Best in Show

Best in Show, a mock documentary that achieved both critical and commercial success, illustrates aspects of Posner's argument, as it satirizes not so much people's affection for dogs as their passion for frothy entertainments and intense competitions. The two narrators of the climactic Mayflower Kennel Club Dog Show broadcast from Philadelphia in *Best in Show*, moreover, simulate not only sportscasters full of wonder and expertise about dogs, but also excited media reporters on a Presidential election night—or at the start of a war.

The dialogue in the United States about humankind's tolerance for reality has focused not only on the public, but also on the government, including its image-making power and its ability to substitute fictive objects for more than a Thanksgiving turkey. Jean Renoir as Octave in *Rules of the Game* (1939), the controversial film he directed on the eve of World War II, asks in exasperation why individuals should be expected to tell the truth when governments and other institutions lie. In the U.S. documentary *Hearts and Minds*, made 35 years after the French government banned *Rules of the Game*, Daniel Ellsberg and others accuse U.S. government leaders of lying about the Vietnam War. The film also accuses American society itself. When, for instance, George M. Cohan's patriotic song, "Over There," sails over images of U.S. forces razing a Vietnamese village, the chilling dissonance suggests that Americans, no doubt along with other peoples, underestimate the devastation of war, and assume too easily the rightness of their cause.

U.S. failure to find either weapons of mass destruction in Iraq or proof of Iraqi collaboration with Al Qaeda on 9/11 cast doubt, of course, on American leaders' depiction of reality as well as their justification for invading Iraq. Had the United States manipulated and exaggerated the evidence for its claims against Iraq? Had it chosen war for reasons it had not acknowledged? In the wake of such questions, a poll concluded in January 2005 by the National Opinion Research Center, University of Chicago, found 31% of the public had "hardly any" confidence in government leaders, and 47% had "only some."[16] Reviewing the lead-up to the Iraq invasion, columnist Frank Rich concluded in *The New York Times* that the Bush administration's "real whys for going to war had . . . [been] replaced by fictional, more salable ones."[17] Elsewhere Mark

Danner wrote, "Never in my experience has frank mendacity so dominated our public life. . . . Our officials believe that power can determine truth [and reality]. . . ."[18] He quoted an oft-cited statement made to a reporter in 2004 by "an unnamed senior adviser to the President": "We're an empire now, and when we act, we create our own reality. And while you're studying that reality judiciously, as you will—we'll act again, creating other new realities, which you can study too, and that's how things will sort out. . . . We're history's actors. . . ." But in this scenario, reality, not just policy, changes as unpredictably as the actors in the cast. When John Negroponte replaced Paul Bremer as head of the Coalition Provisional Authority in Iraq, the newcomer's staff quickly labeled Bremer's people "the illusionists."[19] Speaking in more general terms, senior administration officials in the second half of 2005 informed the press that they were "shedding the *un*reality that dominated [Bush administration policy] at the beginning."[20] Thus reality came to resemble a superficial coat or covering, or something as easily undone by a prefix as by a casting change.

A world experienced as unstable, elusive, fake, and unreal may provoke citizens to seek truth in TV comedy as well as in fiction films like *The Truman Show* and *Best in Show*. "Just how many people are now getting their only TV news from Comedy Central is not clear to me," wrote Thomas Friedman in 2005, "but it is a lot, lot more than you think."[21] "By common consent," observed Frank Rich, "2004 was the year that Jon Stewart's fake news became more reliable for many viewers than real news."[22] That Stewart, star of *The Daily Show*, was chosen to host the 2006 Academy Awards possibly underscored renewed public attention to the world of entertainment as a source of fact-illuminating fiction. Despite the industry's reputation for generating reality-obscuring dreams and fantasies, such films of 2005 as *Brokeback Mountain* (Ang Lee), *The Constant Gardener* (Fernando Meirelles), *Good Night, and Good Luck* (George Clooney), *Munich* (Steven Spielberg), and *Syriana* (Stephen Gaghan) addressed the public's desire—Judge Posner notwithstanding—for greater emotional as well as factual understanding of acute cultural and political tensions. Whether these films indeed made a clearing in Boorstin's "thicket of unreality" remains a separate question.

Tarnation

An extraordinary documentary of recent years that includes film excerpts representing diverse genres and styles is Jonathan Caouette's autobiographical collage, *Tarnation.* Its diverse excerpts from fiction films not only criticize a daily reality he finds maddening as a child and an adolescent, but also inspire him to re-create himself and to transcend his circumstances. Caouette, who stars in *Tarnation* much as Ross McElwee does in *Bright Leaves,* never learns all the facts of his mother's divorce, her incapacitating psychological illnesses, or her maltreatment by parents who, among other things, submitted her as a youth to devastating shock therapy. While Jonathan's mother often finds her personal history too onerous to discuss, Jonathan's grandfather tells him merely that the family was "happy" and that "we love God." Whatever the facts regarding his parents and grandparents, though, Jonathan struggles to overcome grief, bewilderment, and insanity. An incredulous Michael Moore asks early in *Fahrenheit 9/11* whether the climax of the 2000 U.S. Presidential election was just a dream. In *Gunner Palace* (2005, Michael Tucker), which tracks American troops at war in Baghdad, a soldier similarly ponders the line between reality and imagination: ". . . maybe this whole war thing wasn't even true. Maybe it's just burned into my mind now. I'm just imagining it. Who knows?" Yet *Fahrenheit 9/11, Gunner Palace,* and *Bright Leaves,* while citing painful intersections of objective and subjective life, focus on external reality more than inner life, whereas *Tarnation* mounts a sustained, visceral study of Jonathan Caouette's subjectivity or "emerging consciousness."[23] The diverse films he quotes in *Tarnation* presumably helped him both to survive and to fashion art from chaos.

These films include *Blue Velvet* (1986, David Lynch), *Come Back to the Five and Dime, Jimmy Dean, Jimmy Dean* (1982, Robert Altman), *Rosemary's Baby* (1968, Roman Polanski), *Trash* (1970, Paul Morrissey and Andy Warhol), and *My Own Private Idaho* (1991), whose director, Gus Van Sant, served as *Tarnation*'s executive producer. Caouette was likely drawn to major characters in these films, who are rebels and outsiders, as well as to their directors, who rejected Hollywood thematic and stylistic conventions. But even more relevant to his difficult life, perhaps, were the startling overlays in these films of imagination and reality, of subjective and objective seeing.

For the most part, in any case, Caouette relies primarily on his own home movie footage in revisiting his life; even as a child, he clung to his 8mm camera as to a rudder in a storm. *Tarnation* punctuates these home movies of psychic disorder with multiple split screens, abstract images, blank and even burned frames, and abrupt shifts of color and speed of motion. Further,

Caouette's substantial theatrical gifts complement his cinematic agility. *Tarnation* incorporates, for example, Jonathan's brilliant portrayal at age 11 of a whore delivering a saucy monologue bemoaning her abuse and abandonment by her husband. The film also underlines Jonathan's ambition to direct for the stage, noting that he co-directed a high school production inspired by *Blue Velvet*. Throughout *Tarnation*, his multiple talents strive to salvage and memorialize his entire life. Facts and themes central to the whore's report apply also to the experiences of Jonathan and his mother; and one of his chief goals in high school is to create not just any rock musical, but an epic production that focuses on his personal journey. His success in "emerging"—or in knowing, revealing, and refashioning himself—through art and entertainment contrasts to the experience of the father and sons in *Capturing the Friedmans*, whose embrace of performance fails to provide a similar degree of openness and transformation.

Finally, even though *Tarnation* primarily quotes offbeat Hollywood films rather than American avant-garde works in charting Caouette's life, the film's deeply personal form and content invoke the avant-garde, including films by Kenneth Anger, Stan Brakhage, Maya Deren, George Kuchar, and Jack Smith. Not only *Tarnation*'s formal experimentation and non-linear narrative allude to these filmmakers, but also its inward-looking theatricality, its psychodramatic flamboyance. Further, it possesses a surreal and expressionistic air, and harbors an almost romantic hope in cinema as salvation. Such avant-garde currents in *Tarnation* represent yet another aspect of hybrid form in recent documentaries.

ERROL MORRIS'S EMPHASIS ON THE MEDIUM

The influence of American avant-garde cinema figures prominently also in Errol Morris's documentaries, which foreground the film medium as much as the external world. This emphasis on the medium or display as much as the referent is particularly evident in films prior to *The Fog of War* such as *The Thin Blue Line, Fast, Cheap and Out of Control,* and *Mr. Death*. Color, grain, focus, and light shift frequently and unpredictably in these films, as do camera position and the rate of motion on the screen. Blank frames and jump cuts further complicate the view. Moreover, such shifts do not necessarily reflect a specific character's subjectivity any more than they do the external world. Erupting without clear cause or purpose, they subvert the film's flow and narration, and de-naturalize objects, people, and other living things. Yet as these wayward shifts and intrusions recur, they constitute a structure, environment, or state of being. The effect possibly resembles the "music with repetitive structures" or "sonic weather"[24] associated with Philip Glass, who composed scores for *The Thin Blue Line* and *The Fog of War* as well as *The Truman Show* and other films. One might also argue that Morris's shifts and intrusions generate a thicket of filmic reality—a modernist, anti-illusionist environment that stimulates the spectator to consider more closely diverse cultural as well as technical influences on the cinematic representation of events.

One instance of Morris's filmic tinkering occurs early in *Mr. Death*. Fred Leuchter, Jr., a designer of execution systems for prisons throughout the United States, stresses to Morris, his unseen interlocutor, that death by electrocution must be humane and economical. Seated in a bare room, Leuchter evinces calm, reason, moral care, and expertise. Then the film cuts to another space, which contains an electric chair and related machinery, and as Leuchter enters this space, his physical bearing sharply changes. As he walks from one piece of execution technology to another, identifying each in turn, he appears increasingly unstable, not because of his own activity so much as maneuvers of the camera, along with erratic editing and other visual as well as aural changes. Canted and hand-held, with the electric chair central in its view, the camera sets the scene at an angle from the start. Next, as Leuchter plugs an electric cord into an outlet low in the wall, the camera begins swaying more than is necessary to keep him and the action in frame, yielding in tandem with the editing a sense of vertigo and disorientation. When Leuchter announces that he will press the last button in the control console required to operate the electric chair, the film shifts from color to high-contrast black-and-white with deep shadows, and from a medium shot of Leuchter taken from one side of his body to a close-up of his finger viewed from the other side, as his finger presses the final button in slow motion. A longer shot of the finger completing its action follows, in a slight temporal overlap with the previous shot. Both Leuchter's voice and the room noise cease for these two shots. Then the screen goes blank. When the image returns, it reiterates an earlier moment in which Leuchter, prior to pressing the final button, turned the power on with a key. In the next shot he no longer holds the key, however, and he starts to move away from the console. As he proceeds, the canted slow motion persists in high-contrast black-and-white, and denser grain than before thickens the image.[25]

Obviously this scene provides not only a tour of execution machinery by Leuchter, but also a rich display of Morris's technical manipulations: shifts of color, contrast, and grain; changes in camera angle and in the rate of motion or action on the screen; "dead" moments of blank frames and suspensions of sound; time and space jumbled via editing. Although apparently arbitrary as well as unexpected, these technical effects are not necessarily irrelevant to the narrative on the screen. As they exaggerate aspects of Leuchter's appearance, they underscore the horror of the moment. Under their influence, Leuchter does not walk away from the console normally, but drifts off leadenly through the murky air. His eyes become glittery and dazed, his face dark and bristly. His mouth widens into a prolonged, toothy grimace. Thus he comes to appear ghoulish and unhinged. By contrast, in voice-over he continues to sound calm and self-possessed, even while warning against sloppy executions in which excess current cooks the tissue of the "executee" and forces the "meat" to come off, or in which the prisoner returns to life in twenty or thirty minutes, but as a "brain-dead vegetable" to be killed again. The expressionistic visuals undercut the tone of good sense and control in Leuchter's voice that belies the horror he describes.

What more might these aberrant visuals as well as the few odd aural elements portend—and from whose perspective? Might the strange effects indicate that Leuchter is more repelled and frightened by the events described in his voice-over than his tone of voice suggests? One of his vivid childhood experiences was to sit in an electric chair. Do the tremors of that event return now as he identifies with victims of sloppy executions? What other childhood images may plague this son of a prison employee? Do the scene's technical effects betoken guilt gnawing at Leuchter, who considers himself civilized, as he re-examines his defense of capital punishment (a defense he stands by even if the punishment cannot be managed more neatly than in the past)? What about an alternative train of thought: might the technical effects signal not Leuchter's psychic pain and doubt, but his billowing, demonic pleasure as he contemplates unusual punishment and suffering? Yet another interpretive avenue might focus on Morris. Rather than Leuchter's subjectivity, the technical effects might reflect the filmmaker's reaction to the horror Leuchter describes in a tone that is almost too calm and even. Yet Morris is never seen in *Mr. Death*; nor is he heard, except for one brief question he asks Leuchter near the end. Further, almost every film by Morris appears animated by an array of technical effects, a thicket of filmic urgency or reality, which seems to pulse and breathe independently of the film's characters, its plot, and its maker. The sensation that the film is alive, that *it* is reacting to the characters and narrative, leaves the spectator attributing conscience to celluloid or digital video. While some interpretations of the film's technical effects seem more tenable than others, none is certain. The meaning of the aberrant visual and aural elements remains ambiguous.

That Morris's difficult-to-pinpoint strategies substantially diverge from documentary norms has been widely suggested since the success of *The Thin Blue Line* in 1988. Reviewing this film's inquiry into the guilt or innocence of an inmate on death row for allegedly murdering a Dallas police officer, Roger Ebert wrote, "Although he makes documentaries, Morris is much more interested in the spaces between the facts than with the facts themselves."[26] Morris enlivened his investigation of the murder not only with technical or trick effects typical of his work, but also with repeated re-constructions of the murder, enacted by stand-ins. These staged scenes caused the Academy Awards committee to disqualify the film as a documentary,[27] even though staged events had appeared in previous documentaries, including *Nanook of the North* and the British classic, *Night Mail* (1935, Watt and Wright), produced by John Grierson. Contrary to the Oscars committee, both the National Society of Film Critics and the New York Film Critics named *The Thin Blue Line* best documentary, perhaps judging that its hybrid form auspiciously broadened rather than violated documentary norms.

Of course, the film's hybrid form did not simply entail injecting staged scenes in a documentary. More disorienting than the fictive re-enactment of the murder was that it seemed to be repeated almost obsessively, from various viewpoints and with some variations, amid the film's relentless, suspense-building tics and shifts of scale, focus, color, speed, and so on. The overall complexity led reviewers to search for terms that suggested more than "docudrama." Hal Hinson in *The Washington Post* chose "documentary thriller," adding that the film "smudged the distinction between fact and fiction" and that it "keeps asking us to make comparisons between art and reality."[28] Desson Howe of the same newspaper elaborated that *The Thin Blue Line* was "more like a waking nightmare than a docudrama. A true story . . . wrapped in the fictional haze of a surrealistic whodunit, it will leave you in a trance for days . . . takes the hybrid docudrama genre to its outer limits. . . . It's more than fact, and more than fiction."[29]

Reacting to a journalist's query about the divide between fact and fiction, Morris once said, "Movies are movies."[30] Like other contemporary filmmakers, whether their films tend toward fact or fiction, he seeks to recast genre, to go beyond it rather than adhere to standard generic lines.

NOTES

1. Quoted in Frank E. Beaver, *Dictionary of Film Terms* (New York: McGraw-Hill, 1983), p. 97.

2. Daniel J. Boorstin, *THE IMAGE. A Guide to Pseudo-Events in America* (New York: Vintage, 1987), p. 3.

3. Arthur Miller, *On Politics and the Art of Acting* (New York: Viking, 2001), p. 3.

4. Miller, *On Politics*, p. 4.

5. This phrase appears in the introduction to M.M. Bakhtin, *The Dialogic Imagination. Four Essays*, ed. Michael Holquist, trans. by Caryl Emerson and Michael Holquist (Austin: University of Texas Press, 1981), p. xx.

6. Erik Barnouw, *Documentary. A History of the Non-Fiction Film*, 2nd revised edition (New York: Oxford University Press, 1993), p. 348.

7. Bill Nichols, *Introduction to Documentary* (Bloomington: Indiana University Press, 2001), p. 22.

8. See Barry Glassner, *The Culture of Fear: Why Americans Are Afraid of the Wrong Things* (New York: Basic Books, 2000). Glassner appears in *Bowling for Columbine*.

9. Joel Brinkley, "Diplomatic Memo: The Man Behind the Secretary of State's Rock Star Image," *New York Times*, December 5, 2005, p. A3.

10. CNN, November 18, 2005. A news analysis in *The New York Times* one month later indicated that McClellan's statement faithfully reflected the White House position. According to the analysis, ". . . when Representative John Murtha declared that 'it is time to bring the troops home,' the White House lashed out, issuing a statement that Mr. Murtha, a veteran and a hawkish Democrat, was 'endorsing the policy positions of Michael Moore and the extreme liberal wings of the Democratic Party.'" See David E. Sanger, "Path Forward, With Many Ifs," *New York Times*, December 15, 2005, pp. 1, 18.

11. Sanger, "Path Forward," pp. 1, 18.

12. See Randy Kennedy, "IDEAS & TRENDS. My True Story, More or Less, and Maybe Not at All," *New York Times Week in Review*, January 15, 2006. The American Dialect Society early in 2006 voted "truthiness" its most honored Word of the Year for 2005.

13. T. S. Eliot, *The Complete Poems and Plays 1909–1950* (New York: Harcourt Brace, 1980), p. 118.

14. Richard A. Posner, "Bad News," *New York Times Book Review*, July 31, 2005, p. 1.

15. Posner, "Bad News," p. 1.

16. Jim Holt, "The Way We Live Now: Madness About a Method," *New York Times Magazine*, December 11, 2005, p. 25.

17. Frank Rich, OP-ED, *New York Times*, Oct 23, 2005.

18. Mark Danner, "What Are You Going to Do with That?" *New York Review of Books*, LII, no. 11, June 23, 2005, p. 53. The statement Danner quotes by a senior adviser to President Bush appears in Ron Suskind, "Without a Doubt," *New York Times Magazine*, October 17, 2004. Danner also writes about the difficulty of determining reality and truth in the June 9, 2005, *New York Review of Books*. A professor of journalism at University of California, Berkeley, and Henry R. Luce Professor at Bard College, he is author of *Torture and Truth: America, Abu Ghraib, and the War on Terror*.

19. Maureen Dowd, OP-ED, *New York Times*, August 17, 2005.

20. Dowd, OP-ED.

21. Tom Friedman, OP-ED, *New York Times*, May 6, 2005.

22. Frank Rich, OP-ED, *New York Times*, January 9, 2005.

23. A. O. Scott, review of *Tarnation*, *New York Times*, October 5, 2004.

24. These two phrases describing Glass's music appear on his website; "music with repetitive structures" is Glass's own phrase.

25. This description derives from my article, "Errol Morris's Forms of Control," in *Film International* #14, 2005:2, pp. 4–19.

26. Roger Ebert, review of *The Thin Blue Line*, September 16, 1988.

27. For further discussion of the Oscars and *The Thin Blue Line*, see John Pierson, *SPIKE, MIKE, SLACKERS & DYKES: A Guided Tour Across a Decade of American Independent Cinema* (New York: Hyperion Miramax, 1995).

28. Hal Hinson, review of *The Thin Blue Line*, *Washington Post*, September 2, 1988.

29. Desson Howe, review of *The Thin Blue Line*, *Washington Post*, September 2, 1988.

30. Quoted in Sharon Waxman, "Nonfiction Films Turn a Corner," *New York Times*, July 5, 2004, p. B5.

Gangster and Warrior

Hybrid documentaries are not alone in either probing or blurring borders between fact and fiction. While mixing aspects of film noir, the gangster film, and the war film with elements of farce, comedy, melodrama, horror, and tragedy, *Fargo*, *Pulp Fiction*, and *Three Kings* insist that they are based in the actual historical world—typically regarded as documentary's preserve. To go a step further, in presenting what Salman Rushdie might call "new and unexpected combinations" of genre, style, and mood, these fiction films—again, like hybrid documentaries—perhaps advance Rushdie's hope that such combinations reflect and foster richly hybrid dimensions of human consciousness.

In the documentary *The Fog of War: Eleven Lessons from the Life of Robert S. McNamara*, the first lesson McNamara tries to impart in his old age links heightened consciousness to what amounts to new and unexpected complexities, or combinations, of identity: "Empathize with your enemy," he advises. "We must try to put ourselves inside their skin, and look through their eyes just to understand the thoughts behind their decisions and their actions." The psychological (and nearly physical) dexterity prescribed by McNamara seems relevant not only to successful confrontations between enemies at war, but also to the daily advance of civility and peace. While the hybrid films to be discussed in this chapter hardly abjure violence, they share McNamara's regard for complexity of viewpoint such as often forestalls violence in everyday life. It is another way in which these fiction films bear on the world of fact.

FARGO

At the start of *Fargo*, prior to its title and credits, a white-on-black text declares: "This is a true story. The events depicted in this film took place in Minnesota in 1987." The text adds that only the survivors' names have been changed—at their request. Yet no actual "survivor" or other evidence supporting the film's claim to truth has ever surfaced. Roger Ebert wrote in 2000 (in a review of *O Brother, Where Art Thou?*, another film by Joel and Ethan Coen) that the brothers eventually "confided" that *Fargo*'s story was untrue.[1] Why, then, the deliberately false start?

Ethan Coen's introduction to the published screenplay toys with this question before indicating that *Fargo*'s story is fictional. Describing his Russian grandmother and others who journeyed from their homelands to "improbable" destinations, he observes, "They do various improbable things . . . and later tell stories about the things they did, stories having greater and lesser fidelity to truth." He adds, "the stories that are not credible . . . will occasionally turn out to be true, and stories that *are* credible will conversely turn out to be false. Surely young Grandma (itself a paradox) would not have believed anyone telling her that she would never in her life see Kiev, but *would* see The Jolly Troll Smorgasbord and Family Restaurant in Minneapolis." Young Ethan, who was raised in Minnesota, concludes by saying that *Fargo* "aims to be both homey and exotic, and pretends to be true."[2]

"Truth is stranger than fiction," Mark Twain remarked, "but it is because fiction is obliged to stick to possibilities."[3] Perhaps *Fargo* "pretends to be true" in order to break free of probability, if not possibility. In any case, Ethan Coen's screenplay introduction focuses on paradoxical and hybrid aspects of human experience: junctions of truth and incredibility, of homey and exotic things, of the ordinary and its opposite. No surprise, then, that *Fargo*, which begins by testing the divide between fact and fiction, goes on to challenge other generic differences as well. Early on, for instance, when Jerry Lundegaard (William H. Macy) meets two thugs, Carl Showalter (Steve Buscemi) and Gaear Grimsrud (Peter Stormare), at the Jolly Troll Tavern to seal a deal by which they will kidnap his wife for ransom, the generic allusion is to crime and semi-rural film noir. But as the three men bicker over what hour they were supposed to meet, and Jerry stammers lamely in reply to Carl and Gaear's questions about what kind of trouble he is in, and why he doesn't just ask his wife for the money he needs, the film swerves toward comedy.

Almost a laughing matter as well is that Jerry stubbornly overlooks the grave threat his scheme poses to his marriage and to the lives of his wife and son. His tunnel vision augments the film's eerily comic air, which infiltrates even the most violent, horrific scenes. The manner and conduct of Jerry's wife Jean (Kristin Rudrüd) also contribute to the strains of generic dissonance. When Gaear and Carl break into her home, her terror is enacted in self-destructive slapstick, as she ensnares herself in a shower curtain and tumbles madly and blindly down the stairs. Meanwhile, Gaear, who is both comic and villainous, suspends his pursuit of her, interrupting the momentum of the action as he rifles her medicine cabinet for an unguent to treat the mild wound to his hand from the bite she inflicted before she ascended to the shower. Much later, when Jean and her abductors drive up to the remote cabin by the lake, Carl laughs at her moaning and screaming gyrations as—hooded and bound, still mummy-like—she attempts to escape the hoodlums and their car. No Buster Keaton heroine—not even Johnny Gray's beloved Annabelle Lee stuffed into a potato sack in *The General* (1927)—ever had it so bad.

One of the more radical shifts in tone and generic allusion in *Fargo* occurs as a slow pan of a bedroom at night ends on Marge Gunderson (Frances McDormand) and her husband Norm (John Carroll Lynch) peacefully asleep. The shot follows a sequence earlier the same night in which Gaear murders three innocent people on a rural road. His brutal acts vastly intensify *Fargo's* seriocomic tensions; for despite Jerry's wimpy, insidious plotting and the zaniness of Jean's abduction, no one has died up to this point in *Fargo*. Moreover, as Carl and Gaear have sped through the night in the tan Ciera with Jean tied up in the back, a strongly humorous current has persisted—as Carl has complained, for example, that Gaear is a poor companion because he never speaks. But when Gaear shoots a police officer in the head after the officer orders them to stop the car, and the patrolman's gushing blood splatters Carl, *Fargo* vaults into a more ghoulish criminal realm. The gravity intensifies as Gaear takes the wheel to pursue two people in a passing vehicle who have observed Carl hauling the dead officer away from the Ciera. The fleeing car spins off the road and overturns. When Gaear catches up, he fatally shoots first the male occupant as he limps away in the distance, and then the victim's injured female companion, who has been heard breathing painfully, trapped inside the vehicle.

Only at this point does *Fargo* cut to the slow pan of the Gundersons' tranquil bedroom, starting with paintings of a blue-winged teal and a grey mallard,

Even as Carl Showalter (Steve Buscemi) and Gaear Grimsrud (Peter Stormare) play out one of the more gruesome scenes in Fargo, *there is a strong humorous undercurrent to the film with Carl complaining that Gaear's taciturn nature makes him a poor companion. Working Title/Polygram/The Kobal Collection/Bridges, James.*

over which drift the heavy, pacific sounds of the Gundersons breathing and snoring, two people lost to the world in a far different way from the troubled woman just slain with her co-passenger. When a phone call to inform Marge of the murders gets her up, it is not easy to regard this gentle, short, very pregnant woman as the county's police chief, and to accept that a husband and wife can be as perfectly innocent and child-like in their mutual affection as the Gundersons are. As Marge accedes to Norm's insistence that she let him prepare breakfast for her before she sets out in the deep snow to bring evil to its knees, *Fargo* verges into a light parody of provincial goodness and contentment. Simultaneously the film raises the question: Even if there is nothing at all of the murderous Gaear in the Gundersons, might his actions, or Carl's, yet injure their beatitude? Just as Gaear's murder of the heavily breathing woman elides into sounds and images of the Gundersons at home, editing later in *Fargo* links Carl to their bedroom, as his banging on the television to obtain a clear signal at the remote cabin is succeeded by a legible image—of a bark beetle—on the

Gundersons' TV that Marge watches in bed. Thus occur in *Fargo* acute tonal contrasts and superimpositions, involving good and evil, the homey and exotic, and the ordinary and its opposite, such as occupy Ethan Coen in his introduction to the screenplay.

The film's mix of crime and comedy turns horrific again when Wade Gustafson (Harve Presnell), Jean's wealthy father, shoots Carl in the face, after the kidnapper, vexed that Wade rather than Jerry has arrived at the Dayton-Radisson parking ramp to deliver the ransom, shoots Wade. Now Carl's face—hemorrhaging, "suppurating and raw,"[4] and disfigured for the remainder of *Fargo*—evokes sensations of nightmare and monstrosity such as distinguish horror films like *Phantom of the Opera* (1925), *Freaks* (1932, Tod Browning), and *Eyes Without a Face* (1960, Georges Franju). Moreover, not merely Carl's face is deformed, but also his speech. "S" collapses into "sh" in face, Jesus, and *adiós*, for instance, while "t," as in shot and gate, becomes "p" and "ph," respectively. Even Carl's cussing descends into incoherence. Moreover, by this point in *Fargo*, with Carl frantically burying most of the ransom money in the ubiquitous snow where he is unlikely to find it again, unreason appears to rule even when words are legible. Gaear, the man of "wordless looks,"[5] explains when Carl returns that he has killed Jean because "she started shrieking, you know." Next he murders Carl with an ax after they argue over a relatively small sum of money. When Marge arrives on the scene, she finds Gaear recapitulating an action as natural to horror movies as the deformed face, as he grinds Carl's body to bits in a raucous wood-chipping machine that "sprays small wet chunks out the bottom."[6] Gaear forces Carl's leg down with his hands, then with a log.

Marge quickly reaffirms the satisfactions of everyday life when she transports Gaear to jail in the back seat of her police car. Why, she asks incredulously, has he murdered all these people? "There's more to life than a little money, you know. . . . And her ya are, and it's a beautiful day. . . . Well . . . I just don't unnerstand it." Gaear responds with more of his vacant, haunted looks. Perhaps the ultimate horror he poses concerns not merely his refusal to speak, nor the fact that he eludes understanding; yet more fundamental is that he appears devoid of all connection to the world. Performing most actions including murder with blank indifference, he seems irrevocably locked in silence. In *Pulp Fiction*, Mia (Uma Thurman) tells Vincent (John Travolta), "That's when you know you've found somebody special. When you can shut the fuck up for a minute, and comfortably share silence." But Gaear does not share silence; nor does he really hear Marge's affirmations.

While a refusal or inability to be expressive and articulate in *Fargo* does not necessarily betoken disconnection from the world as extreme as Gaear's, it does signal danger. Jerry's evasive stammering, when queried by Carl, Marge, or the loan officer on the phone, loops into his perverse kidnapping scheme, which violates his responsibility to family and society. Carl's elocution, which has been feeble to begin with, declines further after he shoots Wade without due cause and Wade shoots back. Moreover, a running joke in the film is that even people of meager criminal intent are perhaps irresponsibly inexpressive and inarticulate, especially when it comes to describing other people—as in this exchange between a hooker (Larissa Kokernot) who had sex with Carl at the Blue Ox Motel, and Marge, who inquires about Carl's appearance:

Hooker: Well, . . . he was kinda funny-looking.

Marge: In what way?

Hooker: I dunno. Just funny-looking.

Marge: Can you be any more specific?

Hooker: I couldn't really say. He wasn't circumcised.

Marge: Was he funny-looking apart from that?

Hooker: Yah.

Marge: So you were having sex with the little fella, then?

Hooker: Uh-huh.

Marge: Is there anything else you can tell me about him?

Hooker: No. Like I say, he was funny-looking. More'n most people even.

There is a similar dearth of information as Mr. Mohra (Bain Boehlke), a law-abiding bartender and homeowner, reports an encounter with Carl to a Brainerd police officer:

Officer: What'd this guy look like anyways?

Mr. Mohra: Oh, he was a little guy, kinda funny-lookin.'

Officer: Uh-huh—in what way?

Mr. Mohra: Just a general way.

Mr. Mohra's words are unlikely to hasten Carl's arrest and make Brainerd a safer place to live. But they do underscore the limited nature of conversation generally in *Fargo*, even in the case of good, loving souls like Marge and Norm. Obviously there is nothing wrong in the sweet couple's laconic focus on regular meals, fishing, winning a painting contest run by the postal service, and preparing to have a baby in two months. Yet undoubtedly the couple's range of expression is limited, which possibly reflects a lack of experience, imagination, and empathy—a narrowing if not a closing down, a diminishing of human wholeness and connection. One could argue, as at least one philosopher has, that a "whole" person "thinks and wills, and loves, and hates; . . . is strong and weak, sublime and pathetic; good and wicked; . . . in the exultation [as well as the] . . . agony of living. . . ."[7] But such range exceeds the compass and values of *Fargo*'s characters, which may explain why adorable Marge "just don't unnerstand."

Like Tarantino, Joel and Ethan Coen have been accused of making films too absorbed with mixing and reworking antecedent film texts and genres to say very much new and meaningful. "The shallowness of most of their work," one critic complains, "is a result of their creating sealed universes that have few references outside the world of cinema."[8] Another writer warns, "We must remember that the subjects of . . . [Coen] films are never 'the real' but rather other texts and genres."[9] I suggest in contrast that *Fargo*, at least, has a very real subject—the human condition—and that a significant, if only implicit, aspect of the film's "message"—something we insist, in our utilitarian moments, all art impart—is that humanness, or human wholeness, cannot be taken for granted. Rather, in *Fargo* humanness is tenuous, its qualities and dimensions ever shifting, and consequently it needs ongoing attention, needs to be revisited, reworked, and revitalized more than any film genre does. Possibly in probing this reality, *Fargo* tells a true story after all.

PULP FICTION

Jerry Lundegaard, the novice (and nervous) white-collar criminal browbeaten by his wealthy father-in-law, is no match for Marsellus Wallace (Ving Rhames), the swaggering gang lord in *Pulp Fiction* who has wealth, power, and Uma

Thurman's attention. And possibly Carl and Gaear do not measure up to Vincent and Bible-quoting Jules (Samuel L. Jackson), Marsellus's well-paid, well-armed hit men. Yet the text on screen that initiates *Pulp Fiction* is perhaps more modest than the one at the start of *Fargo* (though both films garnered Academy Awards for best original screenplay). Rather than promise a true story, *Pulp Fiction*'s text merely cites a dictionary definition of pulp: "a soft, moist, shapeless mass of matter . . . a magazine containing lurid subject matter and being characteristically printed on rough, unfinished paper." Thus Tarantino's film suggests at the outset that what follows will be cheap, gaudy, amorphous, shocking, sensational, shallow, and undemanding. As if to underscore that the name, *Pulp Fiction*, was meant to caution the spectator against taking the film too seriously, Tarantino has described a pulp fiction novel as one "you could buy for a dime, that you read in the bus while going to work. At work, you would put it in your back pocket, you'd sit on it all day long, and you'd continue reading it on the bus on the way home, and when you finished it you gave it to a friend or you'd throw it in the garbage."[10]

The casual, throwaway connotations of the film's name, as of its introductory text and Tarantino's later comment, recall a title in blue letters during the opening moments of Godard's *Weekend*, a film discussed in the introduction to this book. Godard's title reads, "A FILM FOUND ON A SCRAP-HEAP," and closely follows another title, "A FILM ADRIFT IN THE COSMOS." As is frequently noted, Tarantino named his production company "A Band Apart" after Godard's film entitled *Bande à part* (1964). Both directors explicitly compare their films to scraps and garbage, to things that have lost their utility, purpose, or way. But almost certainly they also regard their films as vital assemblages of such fragments, as mixtures or composts of decaying things that yield new life—there simply is too much positive energy in their work and in their comments to believe otherwise. In making light of *Pulp Fiction*, the film's introductory text perhaps offers the spectator directions that are at once relevant and deceptive, much like titles in Godard's films and the opening text in *Fargo*.

Pulp Fiction does not invoke and combine as many generic modes as Godard does in *Weekend*; nor are the shifts of tone and allusion in Tarantino's film quite so disruptive of narrative logic and flow. Even Godard's titles in *Weekend* seem more distracting as well as more grandiose than those in *Pulp Fiction*. While titles in general have an anti-illusionist effect that interrupts the spectator's absorption in the action and the world on screen, Godard's titles are unusually disruptive because they are particularly numerous and abstract, and their relation to the film's narrative is not always neat and clear. Other examples of titles from *Weekend*, in addition to those cited above, are "DISCONTINUITY," "END OF STORY/END OF CINEMA," "SCENE FROM LIFE IN THE PROVINCES," and "TOTEM AND TABOO." By contrast, *Pulp Fiction*'s relatively few titles identify characters, objects, and temporal changes closely relevant to the story's progress: "VINCENT VEGA AND MARSELLUS WALLACE'S WIFE," "THE GOLD WATCH," "THE BONNIE SITUATION," "NINE MINUTES 37 SECONDS LATER." If Godard's titles attest to their author's broad cultural and philosophical interests, Tarantino's titles betoken a humble storyteller. Yet he too, as a writer and director, has broad interests: *Pulp Fiction* brims with inter-textual references to popular film and television, and with odd generic combinations and jolting shifts of style and tone; moreover, despite the film's flip or casual manner, it is not above (or below) tapping into significant human concerns.

Pulp Fiction's allusions to popular culture are densest at Jackrabbit Slim's, the premiere LA diner where Mia and Vince settle into a booth fashioned from a red 1959 Edsel. Vince orders a Douglas Sirk steak; Mia selects a Durwood Kirby burger with a Martin and Lewis milkshake. Their waiter, who introduces himself as Buddy, simulates Buddy Holly. Replicas of other 1950s celebrities as well as movie scenes and posters abound: "The picture windows don't look out on the street," notes the published screenplay, "but instead, B&W movies of 1950s street scenes play behind them. The waitresses and waiters are made up as replicas of 1950s icons: Marilyn Monroe, Zorro, James Dean, Donna Reed, Martin and Lewis, and The Philip Morris Midget, wait on tables wearing appropriate costumes."[11] A replica of Ed Sullivan, with false Marilyn Monroe at his side, oversees the twist dance contest won by Mia and Vince.

Pulp Fiction's characters come to understand one another as well as the events in their lives by referencing popular culture. Mia tells Vince that some people prefer Elvis, while others prefer the Beatles. "And that choice tells me who you are." Mia's appearance, including her hairdo, suggests she admires Anna Karina, a star in Godard's films in the 1960s, during which time Karina was also Godard's wife. As Jules seeks to calm Yolanda in the final scene while he aims his gun at Pumpkin, her lover and partner in crime with whom she has started to hold up a restaurant and its patrons, Jules refers to the TV series, *Happy Days*, and trusts that Yolanda will understand: "Nobody's gonna hurt anybody," says Jules. "We're gonna be like three Fonzies. And what's Fonzie like?" Yolanda replies tentatively through her tears, "He's cool?" Jules answers, "Correct-amundo. And that's what we're gonna be. . . ." When four bullets fired at Jules and Vince point blank at close range miss them entirely, Jules considers it a miracle, whereas Vince calls it luck, a freak event, and cites an episode of *Cops*, the TV series mocked by Michael Moore in *Bowling for Columbine*: ". . . ever seen that show *Cops*? I was watchin' it once and this cop was on it who was talkin' about this time he got into this gun fight with a guy in a hallway. He unloads on this guy and he doesn't hit nothin'. And these guys were in a hallway. It's a freak, but it happens." Further, when Jules envisions ditching the gangster life in order to move closer to God, he compares himself to the central character in a successful TV series of the early 1970s: ". . . basically, I'm gonna walk the earth," he tells Vince. "You know, like Caine in *Kung Fu*. Just walk from town to town, meet people, get in adventures."

Filmmaker Todd Haynes has addressed the significant role in human development of identification, "that compulsive narrative drive to inhabit what we see." According to psychoanalytical theory, he states, "the ability to identify—to see ourselves outside ourselves—is what first determines the notion of 'self.'"[12] Even if "the ability to identify" is less determining later in life than at first, it remains influential, which may explain why critics and other observers express concern that Tarantino's characters identify unabashedly and almost exclusively with pop cultural figures. Such names as Freud, Mozart, Emily Brontë, and Saint-Just are immensely important to the director of *Weekend*, if not to his major characters, but they have little if any place in *Pulp Fiction*. Possibly this lack of serious or highbrow cultural models hinders the quest of Tarantino's characters, and of filmgoers who identify with them, for a better self, or a better state of being. Yet while the references to popular culture are profuse in *Pulp Fiction*, they do not greatly differ from the sorts of cultural models to which many young Americans turn, perhaps with less deliberation than *Pulp Fiction*'s characters exhibit. Indeed, however problematic their choices of ego ideals or exemplars, *Pulp Fiction*'s characters—more than *Fargo*'s, and perhaps more than most actual people—demonstrate the ability not only to see and reach beyond the self, but also to monitor and reflect upon this process. Further, like so much else in the film, their modes of identification are treated with comic irony—as a game or form of play as well as a fundamental human preoccupation.

Identification as a complex motif in *Pulp Fiction* culminates at the end of the film in Jules's analysis of the way he has identified with distinct character types and dispositions found in the book of Ezekiel 25:17 (perhaps one of the film's few highbrow references), which he has recited from memory before shooting his victims, presumably people who opposed or betrayed Marsellus. He recited the passage before murdering Brett, one of the young men who withheld from Marsellus valuable goods including an attaché case, reminiscent of boxes or cases in *Kiss Me Deadly* (1957, Robert Aldrich) and *Belle de Jour* (1967, Luis Buñuel), which emitted a mysterious light when opened. Jules repeats the passage at film's end as he faces down Yolanda's partner, Pumpkin:

> The path of the righteous man is beset on all sides by the inequities of the selfish and the tyranny of evil men. Blessed is he who, in the name of charity and good will, shepherds the weak through the valley of . . . darkness. For he is truly his brother's keeper and the finder of lost children. And I will strike down upon thee with great vengeance and furious anger those who attempt to poison and destroy my brothers. And you will know I am the Lord when I lay my vengeance upon you.

Jules tells Pumpkin he recited this passage routinely for years. "And if you ever heard it, it meant your ass." But, Jules continues, he "never really questioned what it meant. I thought it was just a coldblooded thing to say. . . ." Now, having been saved by what he regards as divine intervention from bullets fired at him earlier in the day, he finds himself puzzling over the passage's meaning for the first time, and identifying with one character type, then another: ". . . it could mean you're the evil man. And I'm the righteous man," he tells Pumpkin. It could also mean that Jules's gun is the shepherd protecting Jules's "righteous ass." Or, adds Jules, it could mean that Pumpkin is the righteous one, that Jules is the shepherd, and that it is the world "that's evil and selfish." "I'd like that," says Jules. "But that shit ain't the truth. The truth is you're weak. And I'm the tyranny of evil men. But I'm tryin'. I'm trying real hard to be a shepherd."

Jules's journey of analysis and his shifts of identification as he reads Ezekiel encapsulate his struggle to transform himself. As he tells Pumpkin, ordinarily he would shoot him, but he is "in a transitional period," a sort of filmic dissolve or hybrid moment, in which evil and good, tyrant and shepherd, overlap. Jules will spare Pumpkin's life. But, ostensibly to avoid having to shoot him, Jules not only will give him $1,500 of his own money, but also will let him keep the wallets he has stolen at gunpoint from the restaurant's patrons. Further, as Jules's final step before quitting evil, he will meet his commitment to deliver the magical attaché case to his boss Marsellus.

The play of identification in *Pulp Fiction* that engages Jules as he maneuvers to become a new person in a sense pertains to genres as well as to people; in both cases, the "intermingling" and "new . . . combinations" applauded by Salman Rushdie and other artists can be enlivening and transformative. Godard said he set out in *Breathless* to make a gangster film, but ended up with a fairy tale—or perhaps both a gangster film and a fairy tale, much as *Fargo* combines crime, comedy, horror, and the grotesque. Although *Pulp Fiction* is a gangster film, it obviously fiddles with the genre's conventions. For example, Jules forgoes typical gangster goals like achieving material success and ascending to leadership of the gang, choosing instead to emulate a Biblical prophet of 580 B.C. and a peripatetic TV character bearing the curse of Cain. Ordinary gangsters value fine dining and elegant clothing, but Vince dwells on French words for Big Macs and on Dutch condiments that complement french fries; further, both Jules and Vince substitute child wear—used T-shirts and shorts—for their casual but bloodied business attire.

Their imperious boss Marsellus, downed by a car driven by Butch (Bruce Willis), the prize fighter who has double-crossed him by winning the fight he agreed to lose (and incidentally killing his opponent in the ring), staggers more than swaggers after briefly losing consciousness. Rising from the gutter, he starts firing at Butch whose vehicle has crashed across the street. The first shot hits an innocent woman who is trying to help Butch; next the gun goes off accidentally as Marsellus's body collides with a telephone pole; then he fires again while tumbling to the ground. More comic ignominy succeeds this slapstick performance: bellicose Marsellus and Butch are apprehended by the hick, rifle-wielding owner of a nearby pawnshop who proclaims with perverse good sense reminiscent of *Dr. Strangelove*, "Nobody kills anybody in my place of business except me or Zed." Before long his brother Zed, who wears a law badge, commences to rape the tethered Marsellus in a basement torture chamber. After Butch, who has been tied up in adjacent quarters, frees himself and rescues Marsellus, the humiliated gang lord shoots Zed in the groin and

promises, "I'm gonna get medieval on your ass." Then he makes Butch promise never to divulge that Marsellus has been sodomized.

Hence *Pulp Fiction* journeys in the bowels of the pawnshop from black
comedy to horror. Not just Zed and his brother embody crazed instincts, but
also the creature they call Gimp, whom they let out of a cage to giggle ghoul-
ishly over Butch while they have their way with Marsellus next door. The allusion to horror is underscored when Butch, after breaking free, takes stock of
weaponry upstairs with which to wreak vengeance on the brothers and to free
Marsellus. Although he settles on a samurai sword, later a treasured weapon
in *Kill Bill*, he first considers a chainsaw, an engine of destruction preferred in
The Texas Chainsaw Massacre (1974, Tobe Hooper). More gore and horror
arise when Vincent accidentally fires his gun into the face of Brett's cohort in
a car and Jules bitterly complains of having "to pick up itty-bitty pieces of
skull." Other references to horror emerge earlier in the film when Vincent in-
jects adrenalin into Mia's chest after she has taken heroin: as she lies unconscious on the floor, with crusty remains of mucus, vomit, and blood on her
face, Vincent plunges the needle like a stake into a vampire. Scholar Dana
Polan has linked Vincent stabbing Mia to the "The Shape" slaying its victims
in *Halloween* (1978, John Carpenter).[13] Prior to Mia's overdose, the human
replicas in Jackrabbit Slim's impress Vincent as akin to the undead: "It's like a
wax museum with a pulse rate," he observes.

Tarantino's film gestures toward science fiction and magic, along with comic
horror. Posted outside Jackrabbit Slim's, under what the screenplay describes as
a large "neon figure of a cartoon surly cool-cat jackrabbit in a red wind-
breaker,"[14] is the restaurant's slogan: "Next best thing to a time machine." Jules
and Vincent untouched by bullets that have been fired point blank at them
bring to mind exuberant moments of human infallibility, and of freedom from
physical law, in comedies by Mack Sennett and fantasies by Méliès.

Temporal shifts and ambiguities function in tandem with abrupt shifts and
collisions of style, tone, and generic allusion propelling *Pulp Fiction*'s narrative. In the first scene after the credits, for instance, Jules and Vincent drive on
a Hollywood street in a 1974 Chevy urbanely discussing Vincent's impressions
of drugs and fast foods in Europe. Unclear until the film's last scene, though,
is whether the hour is earlier, the same, or later than that of the febrile exchange between the two other criminals, Pumpkin and Yolanda, which pre-
cedes the credits but follows the definition of pulp fiction printed on the blank

screen at the film's start. Equally puzzling, of course, are other narrative questions about the relationship between these two pairs of characters.

Another instance of deliberately fuzzy chronology along with narrative disorientation arises shortly after Vincent's adrenalin injection brings Mia back to life. The action cuts from her home, where he drops her off, to a TV cartoon titled "Speed Racer," and then to a seemingly new character, a boy about five years old, sitting on a living room floor watching television. Two more new characters appear in the room. One apparently is the boy's mother; the other, Captain Koons (Christopher Walken). The new scene possesses an unreal, extreme wide-angle look; the characters as well as the setting appear distended and dream-like. Koons explains he was close to the boy's father when both were prisoners of war in Vietnam, prior to the father's death from dysentery. The captain has evidently come to the modest California home to deliver both a gold watch and a simple, linear account of the watch's long journey: It was carried by the boy's great grandfather in World War I, states Koons, then by his grandfather in World War II. In the Vietnam War, the boy's father and, after he died, Captain Koons, each hid the watch up his ass while in a prison camp to keep it from the enemy. Neither Captain Koons, the mother, or the boy appears elsewhere in the film. But who is the boy? Upon Koons's arrival, the mother addresses the boy once as Butch, thus linking him to the double-crossing prizefighter, called Butch by Marsellus at one point earlier in the film as the two men agreed to fix the fight. Even so, the film's spectator initially may overlook that this boy and the adult prizefighter are one and the same. Other questions concern not only the temporal relation of Koons's visit to the rest of the plot, but also the narrative function of the watch and of Koons's focus on war and warriors. As noted in this book's introduction, Tarantino exulted that the audience would not know at first what to make of the scene.

Events do not become less odd or mysterious as this scene gives way to the next. Throughout his monologue about the gold watch's history, Koons alone dominates the image. Finally he prepares to give the watch to the boy. "Now little man," he says. But the film momentarily freezes into a still frame, and all sound ceases, reinforcing the scene's unnatural quality. Then motion and sound resume, allowing Koons to finish his sentence, ". . . little man, I give this watch to you." As a small hand starts into frame, the action cuts to the adult Butch sleeping flat on a table in his boxing robe and gloves in an anteroom just before a prizefight. Almost instantly he bolts up in a sweat as Mia did earlier when injected with adrenalin (and as The Bride will do in *Kill Bill* at the end of four years in a coma). The screenplay describes Butch as waking up "shaken by the bizarre memory."[15] But imagery that arises in sleep we usually call dream, and we tend to believe that dream even more than memory is shaped by the unconscious, and that it adheres to actuality less literally than memory does. The resemblance to dream as much as to memory of the unreal-looking scene featuring Koons and the watch serves to underscore a major aspect of *Pulp Fiction*'s hybrid constitution. Not just diverse fictional genres, along with various times or tenses—past, present, future, conditional—converge in this film, but also fact and fiction, reality and imagination. As the scene with Koons ends, the dream or memory jams into wakeful reality. The cut from Koons's downward gesture to the adult Butch springing up from sleep yields the sensation of the adult rather than the boy receiving the watch proffered in the memory or dream. Then the first words spoken after Butch sits up support this impression: "It's time, Butch," says his trainer upon entering the room.

Butch replies that he's ready, and heads out to the ring. In the effort to persuade Butch to throw the fight for a pile of money, Marsellus urged him to respect the boundary between fact and fiction: ". . . ability don't last. And your days are just about over. Now that's a hard motherfuckin' fact of life, but it's a fact of life your ass is gonna hafta git realistic about. This business is filled to the brim with unrealistic motherfuckers who thought their ass would age like wine." Like some other characters in *Pulp Fiction*, though, Butch is not easily confined to a single realm, whether factual or fictive, objective or subjective. Instead, in ways large and small, he bucks boundaries and straddles diverse realms and appearances. His getaway in a taxi after he wins the fight he was supposed to lose is staged in a process shot that joins his figure enveloped in an orange glow within the taxi to a rear-screen projection of black-and-white streets visible through the vehicle's rear window. Asleep in the motel where his girlfriend Fabienne has awaited him, Butch appears to dream again, this time of Hell's Angels mowing down Vietnamese soldiers. Again he bolts up, startled, but the violent images are shown to reside in a movie (*The Losers*, 1970) Fabienne is watching on TV rather than in a dream. When he returns to his apartment to retrieve the gold watch, and then as he leaves, sounds of children and of an airplane fill the air, but no child or plane is visible. The sounds that engulf him possibly reside in his memory, or in some other sphere distinct from his immediate physical environment.

Because *Pulp Fiction*'s mixing of diverse genres and of distinct realms of experience often seems whacky and amoral, it is tempting to reject the film as pop-cultural fluff and even as sheer madness. That the film commences with a definition of pulp perhaps invites such a judgment. Aside from pulp, the film asserts links to popular fare such as TV situation comedies and spaghetti Westerns, gangster films, film noir, and cartoons. Again, the allusions are taken to indicate *Pulp Fiction*'s lowbrow if not tawdry nature. Finally, the argument that *Pulp Fiction* ought not be taken seriously is often clinched by referring to its worse than tawdry "displays of unredeemed depravity and violence"[16]—for instance, Mia's drug overdose, the sex and torture in the pawnshop basement, and the chain of cold, graphic killings, often on the heels of humiliating interrogations.

Yet *Pulp Fiction*'s relentless genre mixing and inter-textual referencing call to mind not only cultural products usually considered either base or lowbrow, but also highbrow art—both modern and postmodern—including music, painting, literature, and architecture, as mentioned in this book's introduction. Something similar may be said of *Pulp Fiction*'s play with narrative logic and clarity, as well as with space and time, and of its melding of diverse realms of consciousness like dream, memory, and fantasy. Moreover, significant moral concerns, so often deemed essential to "serious" art, steal into *Pulp Fiction*. One example is Jules's search for God, which, in tandem with Vincent's skepticism, foregrounds not only the dearth of unifying religious beliefs in contemporary life, but also the absence of unifying principles of conduct. If, as a result, human existence feels precarious, fragmented, and incoherent, the difficulty is amplified by a second prominent concern spotlighted in *Pulp Fiction*: the mounting evidence in the last hundred years that humankind will not easily curb its lust for death and killing.

If *Pulp Fiction* addresses such themes irreverently or indirectly, precedent may exist in Dadaist and Surrealist art, which along with other currents of modern artistic expression erupted partly in response to the incredible devastation of World War I. Both Dadaism and Surrealism anticipate *Pulp Fiction*'s assault on reason, order, and norms of morality. The visual distortion employed for Koons's visit to Butch's boyhood home evokes avant-garde imagery from the 1920s on. More to the point, Koons's sudden, almost surreal appearance in the film binds *Pulp Fiction* to the stubborn reality of human destructiveness. Indeed, the tale of the gold watch thrusts the issue of world-wide human violence to the center of the film, and in so doing, it hints at a standard by which to assess *Pulp Fiction*'s fictive violence and depravity. To be sure, Koons speaks of positive things, particularly of how Butch's forebears served their country and loved their sons; without doubt, their example would discourage Butch from heeding Marsellus's advice to forget pride and take the fall. At the same time, Koons's tale, besides making war central to the film, identifies war as a central activity of modern times, coincident with the career of the gold watch, which apparently was worn and activated, perhaps like Butch's forebears, strictly in wartime. In the shadow of the past century's legally sanctioned torture and slaughter, claiming millions of civilian lives, *Pulp Fiction*'s mock violence and depravity amount to mere child's play. At frequent turns, moreover, the film underscores its fictive nature, deflecting the spectator from identifying with the characters, getting absorbed in the plot, or taking events literally. *Pulp Fiction* indeed takes a casual, even irreverent approach to significant moral themes. The film clearly sidesteps the anguish with which Ingmar Bergman, for instance, pondered the silence of God and human destructiveness in films like *The Seventh Seal* (1956), *The Silence* (1963), and *Shame* (1968). *Pulp Fiction* also declines the wry minimalism of the Theatre of the Absurd.[17] Yet the film does pose dire moral and spiritual dilemmas; true to Tarantino's zest for popular hybrid fare, though, it sets them in a context scarcely more funereal than a festival or a carnival.

THREE KINGS

In October 1999, the end of the destructive century etched by Koons, appeared *Three Kings*, another film of multiple genres and allusions that depicts a welter of yearnings—moral and spiritual, carnal and blasphemous—and that greatly expands the carnivalesque impulses of *Pulp Fiction*. Citing the "jarring mixture of tones" in *Three Kings*, one writer has called it "a combination heist comedy, conversion melodrama and combat thriller."[18] This action film set in Iraq in March 1991 at the end of the Gulf War, or "Desert Storm," also includes farce and tragedy in its blend of fact and fiction.

Uses of the camera, editing, and sound in *Three Kings* frequently evoke music videos and TV commercials, but the primary allusion is to journalistic formats, especially on-the-spot news coverage and documentaries along the lines of Direct Cinema in the United States and *cinéma vérité* in France—viscerally immediate nonfiction forms prominent since the 1960s. In *Three Kings* the camera moves rapidly with apparent spontaneity, as though tracking unrehearsed actions and events; at times it pauses or hesitates, as if to locate the narrative hub, and then quickly homes in. The editing is equally restless, darting among various characters and viewpoints. While such rapid-fire techniques evoke documentary realism, other devices betoken a more contrived order and a more subjective, imaginary vision. One oft-cited example of surreal artifice and manipulation is the sudden close-up of colorful internal organs penetrated by a bullet and filling up with green bile, which appears as Sgt. Maj. Archie Gates (George Clooney) describes to his naïve underlings—Sgt. Troy Barlow (Mark Wahlberg), Staff Sgt. Chief Elgin (Ice Cube), and Pfc. Conrad Vig (Spike Jonze)—what actually occurs when a person is shot. The close-up appears in the name of scientific or medical realism, but does so as if by magic, as if an invisible force has shot through the uninjured Barlow's outerwear, which pervades the screen just before and after the infected innards. Almost as magical is the internal close-up of what presumably is Barlow's punctured, bubbling lung when he really is shot later in the film.

Visual images of Barlow, Elgin, and Vig posing in civilian roles both before and after the war are also "inserted" in the film. The "before" images might be subjective flashes of memory that occur to each character following a question to the group from Gates. The images at the end, however, which writer-director David O. Russell has come to regret, simply reflect Russell's omniscient narrative view.[19] Other insertions that seem somewhat artificial and contrived, and that blur lines between mental and physical reality, occur during the Iraqi soldier's interrogation and torture of Barlow. When the Iraqi tells Barlow of the U.S. bombing that maimed the Iraqi's wife and killed his son, the film cuts to silent, slow-motion images of each victim and explosion. But the Iraqi almost certainly has not witnessed these events. The images represent merely what he, or Barlow, might imagine. Then, when the Iraqi invites Barlow to imagine losing *his* wife and infant daughter, purely hypothetical mental images, again in silent slow motion, interrupt physical reality, which here features a bunker and a mode of torture modeled on real places and practices.[20]

Artificial or stylized effects mingle with realistic ones throughout *Three Kings*. Color is often bleached, for instance, or drained to a single value, such as light sepia for the soldiers, tent interiors, and desert early in the film. Action at normal speed veers unpredictably into sputtering slow motion, as when the military officer who berates Gates sails aloft in a helicopter that whips up a small sand storm, felling a pair of chairs. Or, fast motion consumes part but not all of an image, as when sky and clouds suddenly churn above the heads of Gates and Elgin when shooting breaks out between them and Saddam's soldiers in the village housing the Kuwaiti gold. Earlier, as U.S. soldiers wildly celebrate war's end, the seemingly unstoppable action freezes into still photographs of the main characters, with biographical inscriptions affixed to their images. Such manipulated and self-reflexive moments possibly remind spectators that they are watching a movie or construct, while other instants allow them to become absorbed in events on screen as if they were real.

A comparable duality of distance and absorption, of feeling cast out and taken in, pertains to how major characters experience war in *Three Kings*, and constitutes another aspect of this film's hybrid nature. Unlike *Pulp Fiction*, *Three Kings* does not confine its treatment of war to one surreal scene and a few motel television images of Hell's Angels barreling into Vietnamese soldiers. Instead, *Three Kings* focuses on war and its aftermath from first image to last; and a salient theme throughout its rendering of the Gulf War, the first big war after Vietnam, is that U.S. soldiers felt removed and alienated from the battle they were waging. The film's first spoken words, issued by Barlow, underscore the soldier's apartness as well as his perplexity: "Are we shooting people or what?" Later in the film, Barlow's adoring, ill-educated buddy Vig indicates more starkly than he does the sensation of existing outside as much as inside the war, of feeling like a civilian spectator more than a soldier actually engaged in combat: "The only action we saw was on CNN," he says. Yet even the action on CNN, though Vig does not say so, features abstract images devoid of people, such as light streaking from missiles, and explosions in mysterious deserts and darkened cities. TV war correspondent Adriana Cruz (Nora Dunn), perhaps even more immersed than Vig in waves of electronic information that obscure rather than reveal people at war, finds herself similarly alienated: "The war is over," says Cruz, "and I don't fuckin' know what it was about." Her vexation and bewilderment echo Gates's reaction: "I don't even know what we did here." Although Cruz, Gates, and Conrad stop short of adopting cultural theorist Jean Baudrillard's claim that "the Gulf War did not take place,"[21] each individual feels impotent, mystified, estranged from the war and its aftermath.

When Gates, Barlow, Elgin, and Vig settle on a goal they can understand and commit to, it is the illicit one of finding and stealing for themselves and their families the gold taken by Iraq from Kuwait. Eventually superseding this aim is another that is nobler, though no less illicit: saving the Iraqis who have risen up at war's end against the tyrant Saddam Hussein. According to Gates, U.S. President George H.W. Bush encouraged this uprising, but now declines to support it. Hence the double mission of stealing gold *and* protecting Saddam's enemies leaves Gates and company even more out of synch with their own military and civilian leadership than before. Engaged at last, Gates and his cohorts are outlaws. Even worse, by firing on Saddam's soldiers in order to defend his enemies, they re-start the war. Back in the United States, Barlow's wife nails the problem when she hears sounds of a wall exploding over the cell phone Barlow uses to call her from an Iraqi bunker following his capture. "I thought the war was over, honey," she says with a hint of sarcasm, to which he replies sheepishly, "Well it is and it isn't." Gates similarly notes that he and his men are situated on both the wrong and right side of a war that is and isn't: "We killed Iraqi soldiers, broke the peace accord. We're not supposed to be involved in the uprising." His military commander picks up on "involvement" when he declares Gates under arrest for trying to use his status as a U.S. soldier to protect Iraqi refugees crossing into Iran. "We're not involved in this problem here," asserts his superior. "You're way out of line." But in this film, engagement, as opposed to estrangement, often requires that individuals transgress various boundaries rather than stay within lines. In exchange for the Kuwaiti gold that Gates and his men hoped to take home, though not the gold they have given to Iraqi citizens who will remain in Iraq to fight Saddam, Gates persuades his superior to let the refugees pass through the checkpoint into Iran.

A printed statement at the close of *Three Kings* asserts that Gates, Barlow, and Elgin "were honorably discharged" rather than court-martialed "thanks to the reporting of Adriana Cruz." (Vig isn't named, since he was shot dead, and buried near an Islamic shrine amid Islamic prayers.) Summoned by Gates, who previously tried to keep his adventures from her, Cruz arrives in time to broadcast internationally the final lap of the march to the checkpoint. Her frequently muffled voice persists throughout most of the tense, tangled, climactic negotiations between Gates, his superiors, and the men they command. Earlier, in a scene reminiscent of *M*A*S*H* (1971, Robert Altman), Cruz discovered Gates, who had been assigned to serve as her military "escort," fornicating with a rival reporter. When she bitterly complained to

Gates's African American commander, he firmly reminded Gates that theirs was "a media war," a mergence of media and military weapons and strategies. ("Start shooting," Adriana routinely tells her camera operator.) Gates's superior also suggested that if Gates did right by Cruz, she might "hook him up" with U.S. media back home, the implication being that media connections count everywhere, since all reality is mediated, not just the reality of war. Indeed, starting with the film's first images of U.S. soldiers celebrating the ceasefire, Cruz has spoken into a microphone and stared into a camera, rendering an account of the war, and in effect reminding spectators that contact with war often simply means contact with media representations of it, which in turn may be dictated by military fiat. Then, too, the microphone, camera, and camera operator accompanying her throughout *Three Kings* remind the film's audience of the comparable, though more extensive, apparatus underlying the representations of Cruz and all else in the film. This broader apparatus emits its own signals, of course, such as the unnatural shifts of color and motion cited above. The plethora of diverse, overlapping media signals contributes, like Cruz's conflict with Gates, to the film's effervescent humor. In any case, Gates, who is hardly a fool, though he is perhaps too cocky, rightly concludes that Cruz's media presence at the checkpoint and her narration of the standoff could well save him and his men as well as the Iraqi refugees. Earlier he insulted and rejected her. He was one reason Cruz felt "managed," she said, by the military. But finally she and Gates join forces to achieve success in the media war.

Although film and television are highlighted in *Three Kings*, an older mode of representation also appears. Barlow refers to it as "the Iraqi ass map," which Gates, Barlow, Elgin, and Vig, bathed in green electric light inside a tent, interpret as describing the route to the gold stolen by Saddam's forces from Kuwait. Discovered protruding from the rear end of a captured Iraqi soldier, the wrinkled map is plucked by Vig at Barlow's command, thereby instigating much of the film's action. As in Koons's account of the watch in *Pulp Fiction*, then, the ass contains, or points to, golden treasure. Gates detects yet further value in the anal corridor: "You're on the path to truth when you smell shit," he says. If so, it is not merely truth about acquiring wealth; nor is it solely tragic truth—for example, the truth that people, despite their higher potential, kill and torture each other. Rather, it is also comic and farcical truth, which holds that no matter how hard people strive for intellectual and spiritual grandeur, they remain bound to the earth and to bodily needs. In comic films, novels, plays, and other works of art and entertainment, the ass is a locus of human vulnerability, to be kicked, threatened, or exposed, as comedy undercuts human aspiration and self-importance, and mocks hypocrisy, inflexibility, and failed imagination.

In his commentary on the making of *Three Kings* for the DVD of the film, David O. Russell bemoans his attraction to comedy. He avers he set out to make a "studio adventure action film," but was unable to follow the rules. One obstacle, he says, was that the "action that interests me is a messed-up action." Like Tarantino, he finds himself drawn to comic glitches, mishaps, and frailties that in his view undermine "adventure action." With a combination of pride and dismay, he cites examples in *Three Kings*: As Gates and his men charge into the Iraqi compound where Barlow is held prisoner, the momentum is disrupted, though just briefly, when Vig catches a splinter in his hand and calls out. At another critical moment, a character sprains an ankle. Further disruption occurs when Gates, racing through the labyrinth of the Iraqi bunker in search of Barlow, nearly crashes into an Iraqi soldier trying to escape with a pile of new blue jeans.

Whether or not consumerism and commercial ambition are morally objectionable, as a Marxist might claim, to some degree they unite in *Three Kings* the U.S. military and Iraqi troops and rebels, and dampen myths of heroic conduct. A running joke in the film, for instance, is that U.S. and Iraqi armed forces are equally distracted by the question of whether Lexus and Infiniti both make convertibles. Stocked in the Iraqi bunker where Barlow is held captive are not only blue jeans, but also TV's, computers, food blenders, and cell phones (one of which Barlow seizes to call his wife). Not just inanimate objects but also media celebrities like Adriana Cruz arouse intense consumer interest. An Iraqi soldier obviously excited to see her in person, and in this sense to briefly possess her, remarks to his colleague that Cruz is shorter than he imagined while watching her on TV. A leader of the uprising, whose wife is murdered by an Iraqi soldier, boasts of owning cafes and earning a business degree from a U.S. university. Further, good business sense trumps ideals of liberty, justice, and fraternity when Gates tries to acquire a bevy of big, shiny luxury cars in which to transport Iraqis who oppose Saddam Hussein to the Iranian border. He asks a rebel soldier in charge of the vehicles to lend them free for the sake of people everywhere uniting against the tyrant. "Many races, many nations, working together, united!" shouts Gates. But the genial rebel holds out for hard cash.

Besides giving rise to strains of comedy and satire in *Three Kings*, commercial and consumer imperatives underlie at least one grave, didactic scene that is more akin to political cinema and propaganda than to lighter fare. This is the scene cited earlier of Barlow's torture and interrogation. Russell states on the DVD that his impulse toward political critique as much as his love of comedy prevented him from creating a sheer "adventure action" film. Like Gates, Russell was disappointed that the Bush administration encouraged Saddam's opponents to take arms, but then allowed them to be crushed. He concluded that Desert Storm's primary motive was to control Middle East oil rather than to liberate people, whether Kuwaitis or Iraqi Shiites and Kurds. As Russell wrote to a reporter in 2003, "It's the oil, stupid, not the people. We don't care about the people or democracy."[22] Precisely this view of U.S. motivation in Iraq is expressed by Barlow's Iraqi torturer and interrogator as he pours oil down Barlow's throat.

Yet the Iraqi is not entirely free of materialistic motives himself. He acknowledges that he joined Saddam's army for the income it would provide him and his family, whereupon Barlow admits he joined the U.S. military for similar reasons after learning his wife was pregnant. Russell asserts on the DVD that his desire as a writer and director to capture an unusual range of emotion contributed as much as the pull of comedy and political critique to the film's hybrid form; and indeed, as Barlow and his enemy compare notes, their confrontation grows more emotionally complex and more central to the film as a whole. Barlow experiences sorrow and horror at the images of destruction cited earlier in this chapter that accompany the Iraqi's bitter observation, "You bomb my family . . . blow up my home." A further turn and deepening occurs when, in a kind of preface to the imagined destruction of Barlow's family and home cited above, the Iraqi asks, "Can you think how it would feel inside your heart if I bombed your daughter?" *Three Kings* features various parts of the human anatomy, of course: the rear end, where the map to the gold is found; the neck, where the Iraqi soldier trying to surrender at the start of the film is shot by Barlow; Barlow's lung, pierced by a bullet soon after Gates, Elgin, and Vig rescue him; and Vig's eye, injured even before Vig is shot to death. But the Iraqi interrogator focuses on the heart as the home of thought and feeling about what is most precious to us. In so doing, he steers the film toward the question of identification raised perhaps more casually in *Pulp Fiction*: he challenges Barlow to imagine loss such as he has sustained; to identify with him in his heart, although they are enemies; to conceive how he and the Iraqi are the same while also different. A similar challenge to identify with strangers and enemies becomes ever more crucial to Gates, Elgin, and Vig—as well as to Barlow—in the course of *Three Kings*. Barlow comes to understand the perspective of his enemy interrogator, and spares his life when he gets the opportunity to shoot him. Further, whereas Barlow and the three other U.S. soldiers start out alienated and bewildered in this film, and then find in the quest for gold enhanced clarity and commitment, they achieve yet fuller focus and resolve only as they risk their lives and give up their gold for Iraqi rebels and refugees whom they come to "feel," Barlow's Iraqi interrogator would say, in their heart. As if tweaking this theme, a member of the American force arriving at the border checkpoint to stop the refugees from crossing into Iran warns Elgin against helping the wounded Barlow: "Don't worry about him, worry about yourself." But *Three Kings* rejects this isolate stance, opting instead for empathy and engagement.

The film's focus on the political as well as personal impact of empathy and engagement finds echo in the debate about human nature and America's place in the world that runs through U.S. history to the present day. Julia E. Sweig's *Friendly Fire. Losing Friends and Making Enemies in the Anti-American Century*, for instance, warns of the "near inability of the United States to see its power from the perspective of the powerless," and encourages Americans to get better at "seeing ourselves as others see us." In a review of Zweig's book, Robert Wright, a senior fellow at the New America Foundation, notes that while "people in general have trouble putting themselves in the shoes of people whose circumstances differ from theirs," solutions to global problems require precisely such "moral growth." But he acknowledges that there are obstacles to such growth, as noted in a second book he reviews: *America against the World. How We Are Different and Why We Are Disliked*, by Andrew Kohut and Bruce Stokes. Kohut and Stokes state that Americans tend "to downplay the importance of America's relationship to other nations . . . to be indifferent to global issues . . . to lack enthusiasm for multinational efforts and institutions" and to have "an inattentive, self-centeredness unmindful of their country's deepening linkages with other countries."[23]

In any case, that *Three Kings* is not too sentimental despite its message of empathy and engagement perhaps attests to the film's deftness in interweaving multiple genres and tones, no one of which remains dominant very long.

Moreover, the message registers as sober and sound in the face of dangers such as global warming, war, poverty, and disease that call for cooperative action by diverse peoples. Such cooperation undoubtedly requires empathy and engagement—a more complex, or hybrid, human identity that takes into account, even if it does not embrace, enemies and strangers as well as friends. Barlow's Iraqi interrogator indicates the risk of taking the hybrid ideal too far when he condemns American pop star Michael Jackson for being a black man contriving to appear white. The interrogator argues that U.S. hatred of blackness has forced Jackson to suppress fundamental aspects of his identity, and to exist in a state of tragic loss and confusion. This specter of self-erasure in *Three Kings* only underscores the necessity for a more positive hybrid outcome such as Barlow and his friends represent.

A playful variation on the theme of hybrid identity occurs in a wry scene preceding the Iraqi interrogator's denunciation of Michael Jackson. Here Adriana Cruz's rival, whose rowdy sex with Gates Cruz angrily interrupted, interviews a U.S. soldier; and when she asks what as a child he hoped to become, he replies with keen self-satisfaction, "I wanted to be either a veterinarian or a CIA sharpshooter." His smugness betrays no doubt that these career goals are perfectly compatible. Or perhaps the point is simply that, like hybrid cinema, the soldier thrives on incongruity.

NOTES

1. Roger Ebert, review of *O Brother, Where Art Thou?* December 29, 2000.

2. Ethan Coen and Joel Coen, *FARGO* (London: Faber and Faber, 2000), pp. ix–x.

3. *Instant Quotation Dictionary*, ed. Donald Bolander, Dolores Varner, Gary Wright, and Stephanie Greene (Mundelein, Illinois: Career Institute, 1969), p. 259.

4. Coen and Coen, *FARGO*, p. 99.

5. Coen and Coen, *FARGO*, p. 99. "Wordless look" is how the screenplay describes Grimsrud's reaction to Carl's appearance when Carl returns after he has been shot by Wade.

6. Coen and Coen, *FARGO*, p. 104.

7. The philosopher is Benedetto Croce, quoted in Wallace Stevens, *The Necessary Angel. Essays on Reality and Imagination* (New York: Vintage, 1951), p. 16.

8. The critic is Emanuel Levy, quoted in R. Barton Palmer, *Joel and Ethan Coen* (Urbana and Chicago: University of Illinois Press, 2004), p. 50. See Levy, *A Cinema of Outsiders* (New York: New York University Press, 1999), p. 223.

9. Palmer, *Joel and Ethan Cohen*, p. 57.

10. Quoted in Dana Polan, *Pulp Fiction* (London: British Film Institute, 2000), p. 24.

11. Quentin Tarantino, *Pulp Fiction. A Quentin Tarantino Screenplay* (New York: Miramax, 1994), p. 86.

12. Todd Haynes, *Far from Heaven, Safe, Superstar: The Karen Carpenter Story. Three Screenplays* (New York: Grove Press, 2003), p. viii.

13. Polan, *Pulp Fiction*, p. 23.

14. Tarantino, *Pulp Fiction*, p. 51.

15. Tarantino, *Pulp Fiction*, p. 86.

16. Critic Roger Shattuck's phrase is quoted in Polan, *Pulp Fiction*, p. 85. (See Shattuck, "The Alibi of Art: What Baudelaire, Nabokov, and Quentin Tarantino Have in Common," *Los Angeles Times Book Review*, April 26, 1998, p. 3.)

17. See Martin Esslin, *The Theatre of the Absurd* (New York: Anchor, 1969) for analyses of plays by Beckett, Ionesco, and others.

18. David Edelstein, "One Film, Two Wars: 'Three Kings,'" *New York Times*, April 6, 2003, Section 2 ("Arts and Leisure"), p. 1.

19. The director voices his second thoughts about these final images in his DVD commentary regarding *Three Kings*.

20. Russell emphasizes the verisimilitude of both the room and the mode of torture in his DVD commentary on *Three Kings*.

21. This is the English title of Baudrillard's oft-cited book published in 1993.

22. Edelstein, "One Film, Two Wars," p. 18.

23. Robert Wright, "They Hate Us, They Really Hate Us," review of *Friendly Fire*, by Julia E. Sweig, and *America against the World*, by Andrew Kohut and Bruce Stokes, in *New York Times Book Review*, May 14, 2006.

3

Melodrama and Teen Romance

As *Three Kings* comes to an end, tyranny survives in Iraq, more Iraqis are likely to suffer, and some Iraqis abandon their homeland, but the film has its consolations. It leaves open, for example, the hope that the Iraqi expatriates will find greater happiness and security elsewhere than they did in Iraq. And certainly Gates, Barlow, and Elgin are in better shape morally and spiritually at film's end than they were at the start. Indeed, their passage toward empathy and engagement in *Three Kings* lends the film a note of utopian promise and transcendence. Obviously such is not always the case with hybrid cinema (or with hybrid identity). Utopian prospects in both *Blue Velvet* and *Far from Heaven*, two hybrid melodramas to which we now turn, are yet more tenuous than in *Three Kings*. But consistent with melodrama as a form that seeks, according to Linda Williams, "dramatic revelation of moral and emotional truths through a dialectic of pathos and action,"[1] *Blue Velvet* and *Far from Heaven* expose, even if they do not transcend, lineaments of human repression and destructiveness. In addition, characters in *Far from Heaven* posit ways out of these dilemmas, though events defy their vision of a more vital and just world.

BLUE VELVET

Hybrid qualities are prominent throughout *Blue Velvet*, whether one looks to plot, characters, themes, or mise-en-scène. Writer-director David Lynch has said of the film, "It's about a guy who lives in two worlds at the same time, one of which is pleasant and the other dark and terrifying."[2] *Blue Velvet*'s teenage heroine Sandy Williams (Laura Dern), daughter of Detective John Williams (George Dickerson), echoes Lynch's suggestion of two contrasting worlds, one of which is far more pleasant, loving, and lawful than the other. She tells the "guy who lives in two worlds," Jeffrey Beaumont (Kyle MacLachlan), about her dream after meeting him of a dark world devoid of feeling until thousands of robins appear, spreading the "blinding light of love." Manic villain Frank Booth (Dennis Hopper) also alludes to the film's divide between darkness and light. "Now it's dark," he intones following a bout of sexual psychodrama with Dorothy Vallens (Isabella Rossellini), and prior to his attempt to shoot Jeffrey in Dorothy's apartment at film's end.

Dorothy, Frank's victim who lives in ceaseless distress except for brief moments of masochistic pleasure, appears until the film's last scene solely in the night, which is also when Frank seems most active and perverse. Although misfortune in *Blue Velvet* strikes in daylight as well as at night, a darkening screen usually signals ugly developments. Darkness gradually fills the frame, for instance, as the camera moves into the severed ear Jeffrey discovers. A similar frame appears after Jeffrey hits Dorothy, which she implores him to do, and after Frank has Jeffrey hauled out of a car in the night and pummels him until he falls unconscious.

Besides contrasting terror and darkness with light and contentment, Lynch has called *Blue Velvet* "a neighborhood picture,"[3] and his phrase seems apt. Jeffrey finds the severed ear not far from his home, as he walks back from the hospital where he has visited his stricken father. Later, Dorothy introduces Jeffrey to Frank as a friend from the neighborhood; Frank smartly adopts the label, calling Jeffrey "neighbor" for the remainder of *Blue Velvet* much as John Wayne calls Jimmy Stewart "pilgrim" for most of *The Man Who Shot Liberty Valance* (1962, John Ford). Sandy stresses the geographic proximity of *Blue Velvet*'s diverse events and characters in her first meeting with Jeffrey, when she appears before him like an apparition in the night as he emerges from her house on a pleasant street of fine trees and lawns following his second talk with Detective Williams about the severed ear. She quickly informs Jeffrey that she has heard a few things about the ear because her room is just above her father's office in their home. Then, as she tells Jeffrey of Dorothy Vallens, Sandy emphasizes that the apartment building where Vallens lives is "real close to your house" and to "the field where you found the ear." It is in reply to her point about how close together things are that Jeffrey first issues the line that becomes his and Sandy's refrain: "It's a strange world, isn't it?" Sandy then reverts to her point about proximity when Jeffrey requests Dorothy's address: ". . . it's really close by," she says, "that's what's so creepy." It's creepy that odd, contrasting qualities, events, and characters in Lumberton, the teenagers' home town, exist close together, and possibly are so enmeshed as to constitute one mixed or hybrid universe, rather than two or more distinct worlds as Lynch's comment cited at the start of this paragraph might imply. The suggestion of qualities or worlds that are fluid and intermingling, rather than fixed and segregated, seems consistent with another statement Lynch has made regarding his film: "This is the way America is to me. There's a very innocent, naïve quality to life, and there's a horror and a sickness as well. It's everything. . . . there's light and varying degrees of darkness."[4] He has also remarked, though in relation to no particular film, "There is goodness in blue skies and flowers, but another force—a wild pain and decay—also accompanies everything."[5] As *Blue Velvet* demonstrates, Lynch regards nature, not merely civic life in America, as hybrid terrain in which contrary forces, rather than existing separately, converge.

Tensions arising from such convergences persist throughout the film. Even the most sun-filled images are not merely pleasant and cheering, but also disturbing, as is evident in the film's opening moments. For one thing, prior to the start of the story, credits appear over a somber blue velvet background awash with music of restless yearning and suspense as in an Alfred Hitchcock thriller. Then, as the camera tilts down through blue sky in the first narrative image, orange-red flowers rising into frame exert a jarring rather than merely pleasant effect, owing to their intense, contrasting color and definition, rendered all the more dynamic by the camera's motion. Similarly, the white picket fence tilting back and jutting up behind the flowers seems not merely an emblem of small-town or suburban well-being and tranquility; instead, the sharp-pointed white stakes eerily devoid of realistic texture or blemish yield a sensation of imminent impalement. Further, the fireman who smiles and waves to the camera from the running board of a fire truck as it glides down a residential street promises not merely protection from "cosmic darkness," as critic Michel Chion has suggested,[6] but something more ominous. For the friendly man looks mechanical and programmed, with a vacancy of gaze not unlike that of pod characters in the original *Invasion of the Body Snatchers* (1953, Don Siegel). The enigmatic fireman also bears affinity to a billboard image moments later of a woman welcoming visitors to Lumberton by smiling blankly and waving a hand that looks taut and arthritic. Vaguely discordant also is a rectangular shape, perhaps the back of a mirror attached to the fire truck, that almost until the fireman passes out of frame functions as a visual censor, blotting out much of his left arm and hand, which holds the leash to his canine mascot.

Within a few more shots, which include an image of school children crossing a street, appears a man in a fedora, later to be identified as Jeffrey's father, watering his front lawn with a hose. Inside, a woman who will turn out to be Jeffrey's mother silently watches on television a hand holding a gun indoors and moving in the dark toward screen left. The man on the lawn re-appears, still holding the hose and facing screen right. Images of escalating malfunction ensue: water spurts from the joint between hose and spigot; the man, perhaps sensing a reduction of flow (as the victimized gardener does in the Lumières' classic, *Teasing the Gardener* [1895]), yanks the hose, which has caught in a bush; more medium close-ups follow of water spurting and the hose catching and coiling. The man suddenly grabs the back of his neck in pain. His right hand still clutching the hose, he plunges to the muddy ground, choking and gasping. Water from the hose seems to shoot like a sword from his groin; a small, yakking dog drinks and snaps at the blade of water; in longer shot, a toddler approaches the fallen man; on the sound track, mechanical humming and throbbing supplant the music. Next, blades of grass fill the screen; the camera crawls through dense undergrowth, and settles in a dark universe teeming with huge, tussling black bugs. Then the pleasant light of morning returns, illuminating the "Welcome to Lumberton" billboard that contains the smiling, waving, possibly arthritic greeter.

The hybrid label I have attached to *Blue Velvet*'s interplay of contrary forces fits the characters as well as the physical and social universe they occupy. Jeffrey incorporates divergent features of the world before him, as Sandy, who guiltily allows him to court her even though she already has a beau, hints by saying, "I don't know if you're a detective or a pervert." A college freshman with a thirst for worldly knowledge and illicit activity, Jeffrey has returned to Lumberton following his father's impairment to help out at home and in the family's hardware store. He soon finds himself investigating overlapping mysteries, including the severed human ear lined with ants he discovers near his parents' home; the dread and suffering of nightclub singer Dorothy Vallens, who seduces him; and the villainy of Frank Booth, who may have kidnapped Dorothy's husband and child and cut off the husband's ear—and who in any case terrorizes Dorothy by phone and in person. Booth too has hybrid features. He not only adopts a second persona, that of a well-dressed man with an alligator briefcase, but also undergoes radical, unpredictable shifts of mood, often tied to abrupt shifts in how he refers to himself and in how others address him. When, for instance, in a scene frequently cited by commentators, he charges into Dorothy's apartment, as Jeffrey hides in her closet, and Dorothy says, "Hello baby," Frank retorts, "Shut up. It's daddy, you shit head. Where's my bourbon?" But soon he puts a gas mask over his nose, inhales urgently, and proclaims other roles for himself and Dorothy: "Mommy, mommy. . . . Baby wants to fuck." Dorothy replies, "Mommy loves you," whereupon the two undertake sexual maneuvers on the living room floor as Jeffrey furtively observes them through the louvered closet door.

The scene is grotesque, like much of *Blue Velvet*, which won best picture at the Avoriaz Festival of Fantasy Films in 1987. A question arose at the time whether *Blue Velvet* was primarily a work of fantasy, however, rather than a thriller and a mystery. But perhaps most evident in the fevered encounter between Frank and Dorothy, as Jeffrey anxiously looks on, are allusions to Oedipal desires and reversals that in more moderate guise figure prominently in family melodramas. It is true that Frank and Dorothy are anything but members of the bourgeois middle-class often featured in such melodramas, but they substitute for Jeffrey's parents who wait in the wings. The erotic, melodramatic triangle formed by Frank, Dorothy, and Jeffrey casts the latter's return to Lumberton to stand in for his father in the hardware store, and to perform chores around the house such as watering the lawn (precisely what his father was doing when felled by the stroke, heart attack, or, as one writer has suggested, poisonous insect bite), as a kind of Oedipal succession, though Jeffrey has no more dialogue with his reserved mother than his father apparently did.

Moreover, since Dorothy calls Jeffrey by her husband's name, Don, while she leads Jeffrey through lovemaking, he stands in not merely for his father and Frank. Yet another mergence, or at least association, with Don (the man of the missing ear) occurs at the end of the film, as Jeffrey, relaxing on the lawn chair, is visually introduced by a slow camera withdrawal from the dark caverns of his own ear. Jeffrey also substitutes for Sandy's boyfriend, Mike, the football star. Further, the emotional morass of family and neighborly romance grows yet more complicated later in the film when Frank has Jeffrey forced out of the car at the end of their "joyride," as Frank calls it. He then kisses Jeffrey numerous times, smothering Jeffrey's lips in rouge, and repeats lyrics from an audiotape of the song "In Dreams": "You're mine, all mine, forever in dreams."[7] Later, intending to kill Jeffrey in Dorothy's apartment, Frank shouts "pretty, pretty" and "one well-dressed fuckin' man knows where your fuckin'-cute butt is hidin.'" Earlier he has told Jeffrey, "You're like me." Frank behaves toward Jeffrey like both a malevolent lover and a defiant father. After kissing and pressing Jeffrey against the car, and inviting him to feel his muscles, the older man beats Jeffrey and warns he will murder him if Jeffrey persists in trying to defend Dorothy from him: "I'll send you a love letter," Frank tells Jeffrey, by which he means a bullet. The young man finally terminates the rivalry by shooting Frank in Dorothy's apartment in self-defense.

Consistent with the wide-ranging personal traits of characters in *Blue Velvet*, mood-shifting Frank is the film's salient figure of unexplained suffering as well as the chief aggressor. We might well conclude that Dorothy Vallens has gone insane, even to the point of mimicking aspects of Frank's violent sadomasochism, because Frank has hurt and kidnapped her husband and son, and abused and threatened her. But why does Frank, clutching a swatch of blue velvet, display such tearful woe as he sits in the Slow Club observing Dorothy on stage sing of seeing blue velvet through her tears? And why is Frank deeply shaken and sorrowful again at Ben's place as he mouths the lyrics to "In Dreams," a song about "a candy colored clown they call the sandman," which Ben seems to sing (while holding a light bulb as he would a microphone), but that in fact comes from a tape Frank has inserted in a tape player out of frame? The film appears no more concerned to explain Frank's subdued, grief-stricken moments than to account for his frenzied violence. Such contrasting states of being, inevitably interconnected, remain equally mysterious.

Possibly even stranger if less riveting than Frank is the Yellow Man, as Jeffrey calls him. A wary, threatening figure, anonymous almost until the end of the film, he inhabits more narrative roles and worlds than Jeffrey does. The Yellow Man visits Dorothy's apartment early in the film during Jeffrey's first visit there, when Jeffrey has disguised himself as a pest-control technician (perhaps seeking to eradicate primordial black bugs such as appeared when his father collapsed). Dorothy addresses the Yellow Man fearfully, and seems anxious that he leave quickly. The same man, suddenly relaxed and laughing, walks and converses with Frank in front of an Allied moving van as Jeffrey, who has staked out Frank's headquarters in an industrial neighborhood, photographs them. Further, to judge from what Frank later tells Ben, the Yellow Man not only relieves a drug dealer of his holdings, but also participates in the dealer's exposure and execution, perhaps on Frank's behalf as well as that of the town's police department—where the Yellow Man, identified as detective T. R. Gordon, works alongside Sandy's father. Gordon eventually turns up in Williams's home, addressing Williams with an authority and familiarity that understandably unsettle Jeffrey, who has come to pick up Sandy. "Hey, John, get a move on," says Gordon. "Come on, John. Get in gear, pal." Finally, Gordon stands bleeding and probably dead in Dorothy's apartment at the end of the film, steps away from the slain man shorn of an ear, who is usually taken to be Dorothy's husband. Gordon's cold ubiquity, his ability until the film's end to span its diverse worlds with impunity, suggests not only that he may be a double agent, but that these worlds, rather than being separate and opposed to one another, are surprisingly entwined. Sandy's father, Detective Williams, also contributes to the blurring of differences between the film's worlds. A relatively passionless, incommunicative individual who barely reacts when Jeffrey shows him the photograph of Gordon with Frank Booth, Williams remains an odd, suspect guardian of the pleasant world throughout *Blue Velvet*.

Mystery and Education

In the course of this mystery thriller, Jeffrey tells Sandy, "I'm seeing something that was always hidden. I'm involved in a mystery. I'm in the middle of a mystery. And it's all secret." Further, in spying on Frank and his cohorts, in photographing them, and in explaining to Detective Williams what the photographs mean, Jeffrey adopts the modus operandi of L. B. Jefferies (James Stewart), the protagonist in Hitchcock's highly suspenseful *Rear Window* (1954). Lynch was described as "Jimmy Stewart from Mars," incidentally, by a co-producer of his 1981 film, *The Elephant Man*, in recognition that Lynch's films weave grotesque, far-out variations on mainstream American themes and values. Another film of psychological mystery to which *Blue Velvet* alludes—particularly during the brief police search for clues in the small field where Jeffrey has found the ear—is *M* (1931, Fritz Lang). In addition to psychological mystery, however, *Blue Velvet* indeed invokes horror, fantasy, and Surrealist cinema, as one would expect of a winner of the Avoriaz Award. Ants in the severed ear found by Jeffrey bring to mind, for instance, ants in the palm of a startled character's hand in *Un Chien andalou*; surrealistic as well are *Blue Velvet*'s comic overtones and its elliptical, often illogical narrative, much of which remains unexplained to the end.

In addition, *Blue Velvet*'s blend of mystery, thriller, horror, fantasy, the surreal, and the grotesque elides into teenage *Bildungsroman*. Jeffrey declares when he enlists Sandy to help him "get into" Dorothy's apartment that it is worth the risk, weird and crazy as it may seem, for "there are opportunities in life for gaining knowledge and experience." Jeffrey declares he must "sneak in, hide, and observe." Besides observing, of course, he gets hands-on instruction, as Dorothy whispers to him, "my nipple is getting hard," "you can touch it," "feel me," "hit me." Also evident is that Sandy, while uneasy, is aroused by his education, even though she doesn't know half of it, namely the sexual lessons he takes from Dorothy. As Sandy keeps reminding Jeffrey, however, she instigated his education when she stopped him in the night outside her home and piqued his curiosity about Dorothy Vallens.

Well before Sandy drops Mike for Jeffrey, she is unnerved and challenged by how intently Jeffrey observes Dorothy perform at the Slow Club, where the teenagers go for dinner prior to Jeffrey's first exploration of Dorothy's apartment. That the probing of mystery enhances not only Jeffrey's education, but also the romance between him and Sandy, is underscored more than once. Thus, when Jeffrey wants Sandy to help him get into Dorothy's apartment, his words link sleuthing to romance—"I'm going to try and sneak in tonight. It's Friday. Do you have a date?" He means a date with Mike, her boyfriend, but also evident is that if Sandy joins Jeffrey on Friday night, as she does, it will amount to a date with *him*. The youngsters confirm the bonds uniting mystery and romance during a later exchange at Arlene's diner following Jeffrey's line, quoted above, "I'm in the middle of a mystery, and it's all secret." Sandy then comments, "You like mysteries that much"; Jeffrey replies, "Yeah, you're a mystery. I like you very much." He then moves to her side of the table, and they kiss for the first time.

Hybrid Dreaming and Social Order

That *Blue Velvet* is a congeries of genres seems in keeping with Lynch's comment regarding *Lost Highway* (1997), his later examination of home and domestic life: "I don't like pictures that are one genre only. . . ."[8] Further, *Blue Velvet* beckons the spectator to take in all of its generic facets so as to see it whole—a way of seeing Eric Bentley in *The Life of the Drama* recommends in relation to drama on the stage: "And of course there is no reason why the same play should not be seen, now as a melodrama, now as a tragi-comedy, now as something else again, if thereby its inherent qualities are brought out. Reality in this field, as in others, is various and variable, and each perspective on it has some peculiar advantage."[9]

But while *Blue Velvet* invokes multiple genres, it is melodrama that courses through its entirety and blazes almost into self-parody at the end, when Jeffrey Beaumont and Sandy Williams, now perhaps husband and wife, are joined by their respective families—all together for the first time in the film to enjoy a sunny afternoon at home. On the pleasant lawn of this home, Jeffrey and his father accomplish their first and only verbal exchange in *Blue Velvet*: "Feeling much better now," declares the father far off on the bright grass; "Good deal, dad," replies the son. Perhaps in keeping with melodramatic conventions, though it would not be exceptional in horror and other genres as well, the film's end reasserts the primacy of home and family following the evil and chaos personified by Frank Booth. Yet as also may be typical of melodrama, the final sequence is less than fully reassuring about the restoration of order and stability. Indeed, the end's repetition of the opening images, bringing the film full circle, seems quite arbitrary. Here again are the spiky white fence, the bold yellow and red flowers, and the orange-red fire truck with the mechanistic fireman, all of which seem yet more unnatural now than at the start of the film.

Similarly suspect, following the Beaumont-Williams "fraudulent simulation of festivity,"[10] is Dorothy's sunny appearance on a park bench as she embraces her wondrously cheerful, unharmed little boy who, like conversation between Jeffrey and his father, has been absent for the entire film. Where is Dorothy located at this moment in relation to the Beaumont-Williams clan? Having brought Sandy to tears, and having nearly wrecked yet stoked the romance between Sandy and Jeffrey, is she visible and present to anyone but the film's spectator? Or does she, somewhat like the united families, though fully separate from them, exist in a utopian nowhere?

There is also the fake robin, perched before Sandy, Jeffrey, and his aunt on a window ledge in the kitchen, holding a bug in its mouth like the bugs in the bustling underworld that filled the screen after Jeffrey's father collapsed. While robins in Sandy's dream brought light and love, what does this robin augur? Are images of order and contentment at the end of *Blue Velvet* genuine, or do they mock happy endings and portend more violence and chaos? Certainly the words of the final song—audible over Dorothy's embrace of her little boy, the camera's movement through trees into the blue sky, and then the blue velvet filling the screen, as during the opening credits—suits the film's plaintive moments more than it does the upbeat Beaumont-Williams gathering: "And I still can see blue velvet through my tears." Moreover, the recurrence of this song, which introduced the film, brings to mind not just the lustrous order of the beginning, but also the dissonance within that order, and that order's brisk unraveling.

Jeffrey and Sandy repeatedly call the world strange, a term Sandy at one point links to dream, and *Blue Velvet*'s ending is no less strange, unreal, and dream-like than the rest of the film, which seems dedicated more than most hybrid cinema to depicting convergences of dream and actuality. Indeed, *Blue Velvet* could almost be a case study for German director Werner Herzog's proposition—in *Burden of Dreams* (1982), a documentary—that "everyday life is only an illusion behind which hides the reality of dreams." *Blue Velvet*'s resemblance to dream is consistent not only with the film's affinity to Surrealism, fantasy, and horror, but also with its affinity to melodrama. Eric Bentley asserts that the intense emotionality of the child, the neurotic, and the savage, perhaps like that of Frank Booth and Dorothy Vallens, arises in both dreams and melodrama. Melodramatic exaggeration in Bentley's view duplicates the extreme emotions of dreams,[11] while also functioning to "work off" emotions.[12] Peter Brooks too sees a connection between dreams and melodrama, though in asserting that "melodrama regularly simulates the experience of nightmare,"[13] he perhaps focuses on menace and dread more than on longing and desire. Also possible is that *all* films, not merely melodramas and fantasies, are analogous to dreams, as philosophers Susanne Langer and Colin McGinn argue, though each for different reasons.[14]

In any case, *Blue Velvet* points time and again to its dream-like features and to dream as a central fact and metaphor of human experience. When Jeffrey divulges his plan for entering Dorothy's apartment disguised as a pest-control technician, while proposing that Sandy pose as a Jehovah's Witness, Sandy says, "It sounds like a good daydream, but . . . it's too weird." Later she tells him her dream of the robins dispelling darkness with the blinding light of love. And when, after she and Jeffrey have declared their love for each other, she observes the intimacy that nonetheless exists between Dorothy and Jeffrey ("my secret love," Dorothy calls him), Sandy exclaims desperately, "Where is my dream?" Frank Booth, as mentioned earlier, sets his pronouncements of intimacy with Jeffrey—"I walk with you . . . I talk with you . . . you're mine"—in the context of Roy Orbison's song "In Dreams."

Dream-like images throughout the film occur to Jeffrey, or at least are juxtaposed to his image. As he begins an evening walk that ends at Detective Williams's home soon after Jeffrey has discovered the severed ear, for example, a huge close-up of the dirt-strewn ear in dark limbo supplants Jeffrey on screen, and a slow camera move into the ear ends in total darkness, whereupon Jeffrey again appears—standing at Williams's front door. Somewhat ambiguous is whether the ear fading into darkness is a product of Jeffrey's imagination, or whether it is Lynch's directorial insertion in the manner of Sergei Eisenstein, particularly in his films of the 1920s. Similarly ambiguous and less diegetic (i.e., less integral to the space and time of the story) is a candle's flickering flame that appears after Jeffrey hits Dorothy as well as after Frank beats Jeffrey unconscious. On the other hand, not long after Jeffrey's visit to the Williams's home, images appear, such as the swollen face of Jeffrey's father, Frank's face, and then Dorothy hit by Frank, that more definitely occur to Jeffrey, apparently moments before he wakes from sleep.

While no other character in *Blue Velvet* attracts or generates dream images as clearly as Jeffrey does, a dream-like aura pervades the entire film. One reason is indicated by Sandy's reaction, which I cited earlier, to Jeffrey's plan to get into Dorothy's apartment: "It sounds like a good daydream, but . . . it's too weird." *Blue Velvet*'s plot and imagery venture into dream-likeness as events and characters diverge from the norms of everyday waking life and even from most Hollywood fiction, without the film pausing to explain its twists and turns. Precisely what has derailed Jeffrey's father? What is the Yellow Man's relationship to Frank and to Detective Williams? How did Frank and Dorothy become the persons they are? Did Frank really cut off Dorothy's husband's ear? If so, was it his purpose to force Dorothy to join him in bizarre psychodramas, as Jeffrey suggests? Why does Dorothy implore Jeffrey to hurt her?

(Does she not suffer enough already?) Except for the still photograph Jeffrey looks at briefly, Dorothy's kidnapped husband and son, whom Jeffrey and Dorothy never really discuss, remain off-screen for almost the entire film, even when she visits them at Ben's place. Do they really exist? Is it certain, or even probable, that the slain man limply seated in her apartment at the end is her husband; that the child approaching her in the park is her once trauma-tized, now carefree son; and that she has become happy, free of the grief and madness that have consumed her throughout the film? Or is all this but a dream or nightmare shared by Dorothy, Jeffrey, and various neighbors?

In David Lynch's remarks about his life and work, he often returns to his fascination with dreams, in keeping with the dream-likeness not only of *Blue Velvet*, but also of other Lynch films including *Eraserhead* (1977), *Lost Highway*, and *Mulholland Drive* (2001). Of *Blue Velvet*, he has said, "It's like a dream of strange desires wrapped inside a mystery story."[15] Even as a child, he recalls, he looked to dream as an escape into another world: ". . . most of the day was a dream. You can always escape into your mind and slip into a com-pletely different world."[16] Dream for Lynch becomes an overarching term for an age-old idea—the mind as its own place, where emotion and thought are liberated.

A painter himself, Lynch compliments the work of other painters by as-serting that their work transports him into a dream state: "When you see those works, you dream," he says of paintings by Edward Hopper and Francis Ba-con.[17] Lynch also alights on dream when he explains the preference in his own paintings for darkness and blackness, which provoke in him a rich variety of sensations, despite their largely negative associations in *Blue Velvet*: "Black has depth. It's like a little egress; you can go into it, and because it keeps on con-tinuing to be dark, the mind kicks in, and a lot of things that are going on in there become manifest. And you start seeing what you're afraid of. You start seeing what you love, and it becomes like a dream."[18]

He also remarks, "Waking dreams [presumably equivalent to what Sandy Williams calls "daydreams"] are the ones that are important . . . ," for through them one experiences not only escape and freedom, but also more control than in dreams that arise in sleep.[19] On the one hand, then, Lynch seeks liber-ation akin to that sought by Surrealists in their emphasis on dreams and au-tomatic writing, or by Cage and author William Burroughs in the exploration of a wide range of chance operations. Hence Lynch enthuses: ". . . if you could take bits of writing that you did sometime, or even somebody else did some-time, and just chop them up and arrange them at random, and just throw them, you know, like people have done, and then read that, it could be fantas-tic."[20] Yet Lynch will not entirely relinquish either his ego or his control; the freedom he means to assert results in part from his own work and remains to a degree in his own charge. "I'm trying to work inside a dream. If it's real, and if you believe it, you can say almost anything."[21]

In exploring mental life as it intersects the external world, Lynch's films ob-viously participate in a vast cinematic tradition. The U.S. contribution has in-cluded *Meshes of the Afternoon* (1943) and other seminal avant-garde films by Maya Deren; *A Streetcar Named Desire* (1951, Elia Kazan and Tennessee Williams); films by Robert Altman such as *3 Women* (1977) and *Come Back to the Five and Dime, Jimmy Dean, Jimmy Dean* (1982); and, more recently, *Memento* (2000, Christopher Nolan) and *Fight Club* (1999, David Fincher). Rel-evant European films include classics such as *8½* (1963, Federico Fellini), *Last Year at Marienbad* (1961, Alain Resnais and Alain Robbe-Grillet), *Persona* (1966, Ingmar Bergman), and *Belle de Jour* (1967, Luis Buñuel); while signifi-cant instances from Japan include *Ugetsu* (1953, Kenji Mizoguchi) and *Death by Hanging*, the film by Nagisa Oshima cited in the introduction to this book. These films that share a complex tradition are very different from one an-other; a few are explicitly political, for example, and some end more grimly than others. Yet all participate in a major genre or type of film invoked by *Blue Velvet* that might be called the melodrama of mental life.

FAR FROM HEAVEN

Early in *Far from Heaven*, three married women compare notes about sex while completing lunch at the comfortable home of their friend, Cathy Whitaker (Julianne Moore) of Hartford, Connecticut. One guest reports sex-ually obliging her husband once a week, while another reports having to meet her conjugal obligation thrice weekly. Everyone but Cathy giggles. Eleanor (Patricia Clarkson), Cathy's best friend who has raised the subject, trumps the first two respondents by naming a girlfriend whose husband insists on sex nightly—plus three extras on the weekend. "Can you imagine?" exclaims Eleanor, after assuring the once-a-week friend, ". . . you got off easy!" Cathy participates in neither the conversation nor the laughter, possibly because she is too decent as well as too frustrated sexually to find any of this funny. Do these women really regard sex as an imposition rather than a pleasure, or are they just pretending? If they dislike sex, is it because their husbands are inept and ill-mannered? Or is it that the women are estranged from their own instincts and desires, perhaps because the community they are part of—the same that segregates African Americans and outlaws homosexuals—considers diverse feelings and interactions unsafe? And, might this community condition its members to repress or block out not only aspects of themselves but also much of the larger historical world?

If marriage and social respectability require Cathy's friends both to have sex and not to like it, Cathy does not have sex but wants to. In an earlier scene when she approaches her husband Frank (Dennis Quaid) in bed, it is he who does not want sex or sexual affection—at least not with her. Reasons for his reluctance become evident in two scenes immediately prior to Cathy's luncheon. In a movie theatre and then in a "gentlemen's bar," as the screenplay calls it, Frank struggles against his need for homosexual sex after a long day's work as a sales executive. Standing tensely in the rear of the theatre, he catches images from *The Three Faces of Eve* (1957, Nunnally Johnson), a melodrama about a woman with a multiple personality disorder who undergoes psychiatric care to achieve stability and happiness. But Frank's own urges and conflicts, especially as he espies other men stirring in the lobby and setting off on assignations, prevents him from sitting down to enjoy the film for which Joanne Woodward won the 1958 Academy Award for best actress. Indeed, Frank seems even more "un-pleasured" than Cathy, and certainly more so than her lunchtime friends, who have decided either to put up with things or not to know themselves. If only because of the central importance in *Far from Heaven* of Frank's desperation, the film is a melodrama of male as well as female disappointment.

Talking about Feelings

Nevertheless, one might argue that *Far from Heaven* contains more evidence of individuals articulating and acting upon their feelings and desires than does *Blue Velvet*. Jeffrey's father's fury when Jeffrey arrives at his hospital room may be due solely to his inability to speak and to the medical paraphernalia rigidly binding him from neck up, but the question remains open, since neither Jeffrey nor his father ever remarks on this fierce anger. Similarly unaddressed is Jeffrey's mother's frequent silence and benumbed appearance, whether she is watching TV images of imminent violence or sitting beside Jeffrey's aunt at a breakfast table, where she does briefly speak, offering Jeffrey use of the family car. It is the aunt rather than Jeffrey's mother who tries, somewhat comically, to lecture him on the value of family members talking over their problems, but Jeffrey, bearing the physical scars of Frank Booth's punches, cuts her off. Although Jeffrey speaks of his desire to learn about unseen, mysterious things, he says little beyond that, neither analyzing nor discussing his feelings, nor revealing to Sandy or anyone else his liaison with Dorothy. Detective Williams, his wife, and even Sandy are scarcely more communicative than the Beaumonts, and the enigmatic Yellow Man has almost nothing to say. Frank Booth and Dorothy Vallens are bursting with emotion, but they are figures of hysteria, unable to stand far enough outside themselves to analyze their emotions, or to change. The artificial and unreflective manner of members of the two families at the end of *Blue Velvet*, as the pleasant world appears regained or reconstituted, firm up the sense that inhibition and false surfaces dominate the film. Thus, while the fluid convergence of multiple genres in *Blue Velvet* may spark emotional insights in the spectator, the film's characters, despite their many adventures, seem locked in.

In *Far from Heaven* it falls not to the tortured Frank Whitaker, but to a second figure of male frustration, African American Raymond Deagan (Dennis Haysbert), to articulate an alternative to enclosure and falsity. As I mentioned in discussing *Pulp Fiction*, Haynes in his introduction to the *Far from Heaven* screenplay puzzles over the psychoanalytic notion that the "ability to identify— to see ourselves outside ourselves—is what first determines the notion of 'self.'"[22] Raymond takes up this topic in a conversation with Cathy, who employs him as her gardener, when he advocates getting outside the circle of the self, as perhaps the characters in *Blue Velvet* never do. "Sometimes it's the people outside our world we confide in best," Raymond tells Cathy. "Why?" she asks, "Just because they're outside?" Raymond replies, "And because they may have had experiences similar to ours. . . ." Then she says, "And once you do. Confide. Share those experiences with someone. They're no longer really outside, are they?"

The conversation between Cathy and Raymond begins when he notices the wound on her forehead where Frank struck her the previous night. Despite psychiatric treatment to "cure" his homosexuality, Frank was unable to make love to her following a party at their house where he got drunk. Seeking to ease his vexation, Cathy assured him, "You're all men to me, Frank. And *all man!*" whereupon he hit her.

Later in the film, Frank berates Cathy for injuring his male vanity and his reputation as a business leader by associating with Raymond. Although this association has been platonic, she decides to break it off, and phones Raymond to request a meeting. In front of the same theatre where Frank was distracted from watching *The Three Faces of Eve*, Cathy and Raymond resume their conversation about individuals venturing outside their personal and social worlds. When Cathy says she has been "reckless and foolish" to think the community would allow her and Raymond to enjoy any relationship at all, he insists, through a series of rhetorical questions, that it is anything but wrong to believe "that one person could reach out to another, take an interest in another. And that maybe, for one fleeting instant, could manage to see beyond the surface—beyond the color of things." Cathy asks, "Do you think we ever really do? See beyond these things? The surface of things?" He responds, ". . . Yes I do. I don't really have a choice," to which she can only say, "I wish I could."

Bridging Differences

Such thoughts about going beyond surfaces, reaching out to other individuals, sharing different yet similar experiences, and altering the definition of outside and in, obviously bear on what occurs between Barlow and his Iraqi interrogator in *Three Kings* and on the experience of all four American heroes in that film. While these thoughts are commonplace in some quarters, they are unusual and even sacrilegious in *Far-from-Heaven* Hartford. According to Raymond and Cathy, at least one additional step in unlocking the self by making connections outside it entails focusing on matters of feeling and identification, which also concern Jules in *Pulp Fiction* as well as Barlow's interrogator in *Three Kings*. Moments after Cathy suggests to Raymond that once you share an experience with another person, that person is "no longer really outside," she recalls discovering Raymond to be the only black person, along with his daughter, at the opening of a big Harford art exhibit attended by Cathy and her chums: ". . . I just kept wondering what it must be like. Being the only one in the room. Colored, or whatever, it was. How that might possibly feel," she says. Raymond replies that there is a "part of Harford where everybody does indeed look like me. Only trouble is, very few people ever

Raymond Deagan (Dennis Haysbert) and his daughter are the only African Americans at a gallery opening in Hartford in Far from Heaven. *Later Cathy Whitaker (Julianne Moore) accompanies Raymond to a restaurant in the African American part of town where she is the only Caucasian in the room. Killer Films/The Kobal Collection/Genser, Abbot.*

leave that world." He then invites Cathy to a restaurant in his part of town where Cathy becomes "the only one," and where they are spotted entering by one of Hartford's upstanding, gossipy women, who is visiting the neighborhood to get her car washed.

Later, Cathy returns to the topic of feeling, again in relation to Raymond, when she informs her best friend Eleanor of Frank's homosexuality and his decision to leave her for a young blond boy he has met while vacationing with Cathy in Miami. After explaining that "what's been hardest of all" in her ordeal with Frank is "the endless secrecy, our entire lives just—shut in the dark," Cathy shocks Eleanor by confiding that Raymond has been the "only person" she could talk to: "Somehow it made me feel—oh, I don't know. Alive somewhere." Moreover, when Cathy raises the issue of feeling for the first time, it is in a conversation with Raymond, as she tries to describe to him, during their chance encounter at the big art exhibit, her reaction to a work by Joan Miró: "I don't know why but I just adore it. The feeling it gives. I know that sounds terribly vague." Raymond replies by linking her comment to his theory that modern art seeks to "somehow show you divinity," though more abstractly than religious art once did. Whatever the logical merits of his argument, it locates spiritual value both in her adoration of art and, more generally, in her ability to feel and to talk about feeling.

At the same time, the difficulty of acknowledging and explaining feeling is evident throughout the film. Only when Frank meets with a psychiatrist does he speak at last of his self-loathing, though he remains silent about society's possible responsibility for the view he holds of himself. That Frank's needs choke and stifle him is suggested also when Cathy tells him, as she dances with him during their Miami vacation, that he looks "fetching" in his tuxedo and tie, and he responds, "I can hardly breathe in it." Only at the end, in asking Cathy for a divorce, does he express joy as well as his true need, and only then does he believe himself to be loved by someone he desires sexually. The irony is that the blond young man he has met in Miami, with whom he now lives, seems too cold and self-involved to justify Frank's hope of enduring love.

Cathy stresses her own stifling circumstances when she admits to Eleanor that she has lived in "endless secrecy . . . shut in the dark." Even her sympathy for Frank earlier in the film seems largely to have masked her anguish over his physical and emotional distance. The pervasiveness of disguise, secrecy, suppression, and self-denial in *Far from Heaven* is summed up in falsely playful tones by Cathy and Frank during the party at their house. When a male friend of the couple speaks admiringly of Cathy's beauty, Frank drunkenly snorts, "Smoke and mirrors. . . . You should see her without her face on!" Cathy swiftly adds, "We ladies are never really what we appear . . . every girl has her secrets!"

Cathy's best friend Eleanor reinforces the pattern of repression. Before learning of Frank's sexuality, Eleanor admits to not liking homosexuals, but also to not knowing any. "I just like all the men I'm around to be all men," she tells Cathy, a thought Cathy tries out during her aborted sex with Frank at the end of the party. After Cathy converses with Raymond at the art exhibit, Eleanor rushes up to her in a panic: "You have the whole place in a clamor!" And when Cathy confesses to Eleanor her feeling for Raymond, her best friend will not hear of it.

Nor, unfortunately, will Raymond at film's end. His daughter has nearly been stoned to death by white male playmates poisoned by the town's reaction to his friendship with Cathy. "Colored" people have taken to hurling rocks through the windows of his home. He believed in reaching out to other people who were both different and similar to himself—reaching out until, as Cathy said, the other was no longer outside. Now that commitment has failed. A chastened Raymond has boarded up several windows of his home, and prepares to leave Hartford, explaining to Cathy, "I've learned my lesson about mixing with other worlds. . . . I've seen the sparks fly. . . . All kinds."

Contending with "Authority"

Evident in Todd Haynes's introduction to the published screenplay as well as in the film itself is that Haynes considers *Far from Heaven* a social critique in the tradition of film melodramas by Douglas Sirk and Max Ophuls. Beneath the "teeming surfaces" of their films, he explains, "are claustrophobic stories of disillusionment and resignation, of women locked up in houses who emerge, in the end, as lesser human beings for all they surrender to the ways of the world."[23] He also writes, "The most beautiful melodramas, like those of Sirk and Ophuls, are the ones that show how the worlds in which these characters live—and the happy endings foisted upon them—are wrong."[24] Similarly, Haynes finds in three of his own "women's films"—*Superstar: The Karen Carpenter Story* (1987), *Safe* (1995), and *Far from Heaven*—"women struggling within the constraints of domestic life, each of whom surrenders . . . to its authority."[25] He adds that his three films about struggling women, like the films of Sirk and Ophuls, "articulate emotion through the corridors of style."[26] And then he says that he "first conceived *Far from Heaven* as a tribute to Douglas Sirk. This was my chance," he asserts, "to study the intricacy and boldness of classic form; the lush, sculptural style and sublime emotionality of films like *All that Heaven Allows* (1956), *Written on the Wind* (1957), and *Imitation of Life* (1960)."[27] Valuing Sirk's melodramas for presenting sad social truths with unique stylistic flair, then, Haynes created in *Far from Heaven* an unusual hybrid film—one that alludes, or looks outside itself, to one other film in particular, *All that Heaven Allows*.

Of course, *Far from Heaven* alludes also to films other than *All that Heaven Allows*. As I mentioned before, Frank Whitaker views a scene in *Three Faces of Eve*, in which, states Haynes's screenplay, "Raymond Burr is questioning one of Joanne Woodward's more timid personalities [and] Woodward . . . becoming agitated . . . starts switching into another personality."[28] *Far from Heaven* also refers to *Hilda Crane* (1956, Philip Dunne), a melodrama about a woman who must choose between two very different men, which appeared the same year as *All that Heaven Allows*. As Cathy, after Frank's tantrum over rumors of her friendship with Raymond, tells Raymond she will no longer see him, she and her friend stand outside the movie theatre Frank previously visited; and occupying the top line on the marquee above them is the title, *Hilda Crane*.

In addition, it may not be farfetched to see in *Far from Heaven* an allusion to a celebrated silent film, *The Last Laugh* (1924, F. W. Murnau), when Cathy bears food to her husband whom she believes to be working late at his office downtown. After passing through a revolving door of shimmering glass, taking an elevator, and arriving at his office to find Frank in erotic embrace with a man, she recoils and runs off. The moment resembles a scene in Murnau's film in which the daft wife of the proud old doorman at the luxury hotel in Berlin pays him a surprise visit to bring him food. Approaching the revolving door to the hotel, she finds a younger man in her husband's martial-looking uniform and occupying his place at the door; next she discovers her husband, stripped of all authority, tending the lavatory in the hotel basement. Feeling debased and repelled, she recoils like Cathy does, and hastens away. In a previous scene the doorman himself recoils, when prior to officially learning of his demotion, he finds the uniformed younger man, erect and imperious, guarding the re-volving door. Both *Far from Heaven* and *The Last Laugh* thus render scenes of shock and loss involving a workplace, social status, and marriage—with a package of food and a revolving door as key objects.

Regarding *Far from Heaven*'s primary allegiance to *All that Heaven Allows*, Haynes, in his commentary on the *Far from Heaven* DVD, praises Sirk's cam-era, mise-en-scène, and music as "creating emotion" and "speaking" for char-acters since "words fail us." Yet such expressive uses of cinematic style are not unique to Sirk, or to melodrama, but are central to film practice in general. Murnau himself was a master at making the mobile camera, lighting, and other elements of mise-en-scène "speak." Further, the German cinematic tra-dition, renowned for its technical and psychological skills in merging expres-sionism and realism, undoubtedly influenced Sirk, who wrote and directed films in Germany before moving to Hollywood. Perhaps it is a further mea-sure of Haynes's esteem for Sirk that he casts the director of *All that Heaven Allows* as representative of a vast historical tradition. In any case, while *Far from Heaven* alludes to films other than Sirk's, it adheres most insistently, from its first frame on, to aspects of plot, theme, character, and mise-en-scène in

Sirk's *All that Heaven Allows*. Whereas hybrid films such as *Blue Velvet, Pulp Fiction*, and *Kill Bill* restlessly allude to one film or genre and then to another, *Far from Heaven* sticks primarily to one work, and thereby testifies more than words can say to Haynes's respect for its director.

Parallels between *All that Heaven Allows* and *Far from Heaven* abound. Perhaps to indicate that she is readier than she admits to cease mourning for her late husband, Sirk's middle-aged heroine Cary Scott (Jane Wyman) dons an orange dress, prompting her son to accuse her of immodesty—a charge her daughter rejects as a "typical Oedipus reaction." Later, when Howard, a married friend, makes a play for Cary at a party, she is bathed in orange light, though he is not. Cathy Whitaker's giggling guests at lunch who complain of the sexual costs of marriage also wear orange, a color Cathy in her frustration occasionally wears as well. As two characters converse in *All that Heaven Allows*, darkness often obscures the face of one but not of the other, possibly suggesting dissonance or discord between their respective perceptions and desires. The face of the doctor who dismays Cary by telling her she was ready for a love affair with Ron Kirby (Rock Hudson), but not for love, resides in dense shadow except for his ear. One of the few times Cary and Ron appear to be equally and fully lit occurs in the final scene when, after Ron has been critically injured, Cary stops resisting her desire to be with him, and stands by him in his home. Comparable tensions of light and dark arise in *Far from Heaven*—for example, when Frank Whitaker exposes his troubled sexuality amid the flickering neon downtown at night, where he finds a seedy movie theatre, and then a gentlemen's bar. Haynes's occasionally canted camera in this sequence lends Frank's desires an aggressive thrust. Later, when Frank arrives home from work drunk and enraged because Cathy has been associating with Raymond, and because Frank himself has been suspended from his job, darkness shrouds his angry, crumbling figure in the hallway, while Cathy's forlorn face remains clearly visible.

Light is key toward the end of the film as well, when Frank arrives home again, starts to weep, and tells Cathy he has "fallen in love with someone." In this dialogue between husband and wife, semi-transparent curtains over the windows, along with the indefinite quality of the light outside, leave more open than elsewhere in the film the question of whether the time is night or day. Such ambiguity seems appropriate because Frank's revelation—not only that he has fallen in love, but that he has never known this feeling before— shatters the couple's world including their usual experience of space and time.

The relation of curtains to light figures yet again, incidentally, when Frank phones Cathy at night to set a time for signing the divorce papers. In Frank's hotel room, where his blond partner in bed appears indifferent to Frank's negotiation with Cathy, opaque, thick curtains hang utterly still, while thinner, suppler, more transparent curtains in Cathy's bedroom, as she takes Frank's call, move gently, as if trembling.

In addition to broad similarities, there are major differences in how *Far from Heaven* and *All that Heaven Allows* approach character, plot, theme, and mise-en-scène. Both films start, for example, with the camera stationed high, near a large clock on a stone tower, peering down on a town; then the camera pans in each film and descends slowly on a "fall day . . . alive with . . . autumn reds and golds"[29] until it tracks above a station wagon driven by the heroine. But while Haynes's high-angle view at the start of the film incorporates a train station downtown, Sirk's camera frames a church spire and children playing on a grassy square. At the outset, the world of the later film seems somewhat more urban, commercial, and industrial than Sirk's. Further, the camera soon moves more fluidly in Haynes's universe of imminent social change than in Sirk's more fixed community. Sirk's Cary Scott is given a television by her children to relieve her loneliness, but it is never turned on. No news of the outside world appears on its screen—just reflections of Cary's sad face and of flames in her fireplace. In the Whitaker household, on the other hand, President Dwight D. Eisenhower appears on television calling for the integration of Little Rock's schools, an executive action that will prompt Hartford's elite to weigh the likelihood of similar changes hitting their city.

While Sirk's heroine Cary is a widow, Cathy Whitaker is not. Even though Cathy's husband is alive, however, he is either physically or emotionally absent from their home most of the time. Both Cary and Cathy choose as lovers, or potential lovers, men forbidden to them by society. Cary's peers and college-age progeny consider Ron Kirby, who resides outside of town, and who trims trees and runs a nursery for a living, too young and low-class for her. In the case of Cathy's choices, Raymond and Frank, the focus of criticism shifts from age and class to race and something else. The African American gardener, who replicates Ron's vocation and affection for nature, is deemed unfit racially; while Frank, who has no counterpart in Sirk's film, must be distanced immediately, says Eleanor when she discovers his homosexuality, lest his malady infect his children. Cathy's friends ignore that Raymond is a responsible and

loving father and that Frank is not; they also ignore that Raymond is unusually sensitive and articulate, whether compared to other characters in *Far from
Heaven* or to Ron Kirby. A further difference between the two films is that *Far
from Heaven* presents in Frank not only a tormented homosexual but also, far
more than Ron Kirby, an exemplar of that overwrought emotion frequently
cited as key to melodrama, where it is commonly located in women, however,
rather than in men.[30]

In simultaneously emulating and diverging from *All that Heaven Allows*,
Far from Heaven takes a path resembling that posited by Raymond and Cathy
in the most ideal moments of their relationship. Much as these characters
contemplate reaching out to people who are both different and similar to
themselves, penetrating the surfaces of things, sharing emotions and under-
standings, altering the divide between outside and in, Haynes reaches out to
a similar yet different film made before he was born. Entering into *All that
Heaven Allows* and the historical moment in which it was created, while simultaneously drawing that film and its era into the present, *Far from Heaven*
inclines toward connection rather than isolation.

Such a disposition distinguishes most hybrid films, of course, since they
repeatedly acknowledge the inspiration of other films, genres, artists, and
audiences—both past and present. Hybrid films may satirize such influences,
as *Fargo* does; or like *Kill Bill, Pulp Fiction, Tarnation, Atomic Café,* and Godard's *Weekend,* they may allude to so many works of diverse moods and looks
as to create an explosive rather than meditative air, a maximal transgression of
limits, a sort of anti-form. Further, such hybrid films may thereby assert dom-
inance over their influences more than indebtedness to them. *Far from Heaven*
takes another tack: rather than satirize, transgress, or upstage its sources, it
emulates and adapts what Haynes has called "the intricacy and boldness of
classic form"[31] found in Sirk's vision of melodrama.

Probably *Far from Heaven*'s studious, graceful engagement with one work in
particular would have been less feasible had Haynes not believed in the social
and political (as well as artistic) boldness of *All that Heaven Allows* and of the
genre it represents. This boldness would seem to reside at least partially for
Haynes in the ability of melodrama to examine human repression and destructiveness, as posited at the start of this chapter. He quotes Rainer Werner
Fassbinder, the German filmmaker who in 1974 made *Fear Eats the Soul,* which
like Haynes's film drew inspiration from *All that Heaven Allows*: "Revolution

doesn't belong on the cinema screen," said Fassbinder, "but outside, in the world."[32] But Haynes agrees when Fassbinder also asserts that films can explore "certain [social, political, and cultural] mechanisms clearly enough to show people how they work," and thereby spur spectators to mobilize what Haynes calls their "extraordinary powers . . . to reflect (upon) themselves" and to transform their lives.[33] In paralleling *All that Heaven Allows*, then, *Far from Heaven* dedicates itself not simply to this particular film but to the ongoing quest for human betterment.

POISON

Although in adopting hybrid form and highlighting repression, *Blue Velvet* and *Far from Heaven* diverge from much mainstream cinema, both films gained Hollywood honors, with *Far from Heaven* receiving four academy award nominations, including one for Haynes's screenplay, while Lynch won a nomination for best director. Yet more radically hybrid than either film, as well as harsher in its view of society, is Haynes's early feature, *Poison* (1991), which received no academy award nomination, but won best picture at both the Sundance Film Festival and the Berlin International Film Festival.

In a tour de force of crosscutting harking back to tactics in D. W. Griffith's more epic, less intimate film, *Intolerance, Poison* interweaves three distinct stories, each alluding to a different genre: "Horror," a science fiction spoof, features an ambitious young researcher, Dr. Thomas Graves (Larry Maxwell), determined, as he explains, to "capture the sex drive." But as he observes Dr. Nancy Olson's (Susan Norman) fetching gait after she applies to be his assistant, Graves absent-mindedly drinks a sexual potion he has formulated, which transforms him into a leprous mutant who starts a deadly epidemic. "Hero," a mock documentary about Richie Beacon (Chris Singh), a seven-year-old boy who vanishes into thin air after fatally shooting his father one night to stop him from beating the boy's mother, consists mainly of fake interviews with Richie's grateful, surviving parent as well as others who knew him, such as friends, teachers, and a nurse; "Homo" is simultaneously a prison film and an account of increasingly tortured love between two homosexual prison inmates, John Broom (Scott Renderer) and Jack Bolton (James Lyons), who first meet as teenagers in a reformatory. "Homo" inter-cuts dimly-lit prison scenes with sunny images of youthful romance.

Bolton dies at the end of "Homo" as he tries to escape prison. Graves fatally jumps at the end of "Horror" into a mob too angry and fearful to remember he did not *choose* to become leprous. Also, *Poison* begins with the apparent discovery of a death—probably that of Nancy Olson in her apartment. Moreover, the entire train of death, fear, and physical violence in *Poison* seems instigated by sexual desire. In "Hero," Fred Beacon (Edward Allen) probably beats Richie's mother Felicia (Edith Meeks) because she has been sleeping with their Hispanic gardener. (Then again, Fred also beats Richie routinely.) Further unifying *Poison*'s three stories is the strain of melodramatic excess, involving not only exorbitant emotion, violence, and one-dimensional characters, but also stylistic extremes such as the high-contrast black-and-white and oblique camera positions in "Horror."

Further, the three stories as well as their central male characters converge as a result of the way the film is edited. For example, *Poison*'s first two scenes closely juxtapose an apparent death in Olson's apartment and the announcement, at the start of "Hero," that Richie Beacon has committed patricide. Moreover, the first scene in Olson's apartment concludes with police and neighbors peering down a corridor toward an open window through which someone—possibly a killer—has fled. The hand-held moving camera then proceeds down the corridor and out the window into empty space, where the scene ends. In the "Hero" sequence that immediately follows, the voice-over announcing the father's death states that Mrs. Beacon observed her son, after the slaying, "take off in flight from the patio balcony" and vanish into the air. The visual and verbal references both to death and to escapes and vanishings link together the first sequences of "Horror" and "Hero." It is almost as if one and the same person, who is never visible to the film's spectator, escapes in both stories quite magically, like a phantom. At the end of the introduction to "Hero," the voice-over, having summarized Richie Beacon's grim deed and escape, asks, "Who was Richie Beacon and where is he now?" "Homo" then begins with a close-up of a young boy's hand carefully making its way in the dark over a piece of furniture and then stealthily reaching for items in a drawer. The spectator might easily infer that this image answers the question of Richie Beacon's whereabouts—and possibly of his nature or identity as well. Yet the hand turns out to be John Broom's as a child—already a thief—not Richie's. Such ambiguity promoted by editing persists throughout *Poison*'s three stories, blurring borders of plot and identity, and merging allusions to diverse genres as well.

NOTES

1. Quoted in Barry Langford, *Film Genre: Hollywood and Beyond* (Edinburgh: Edinburgh University Press, 2005), p. 31; see Linda Williams, "Melodrama Revised," in Nick Browne (ed.), *Refiguring American Film Genres* (Berkeley: University of California Press, 1998), pp. 42–88.

2. Quoted in Michel Chion, *David Lynch*, trans. Robert Julian (London: British Film Institute, 1995), p. 84.

3. David Lynch, *Lynch on Lynch*, ed. Chris Rodley (London: Faber and Faber, 1997), p. 138.

4. Lynch, *Lynch on Lynch*, p. 139.

5. Lynch, *Lynch on Lynch*, p. 8.

6. Chion, *David Lynch*, p. 83.

7. These are the words I jotted down while viewing the film. But the lyrics for Roy Orbison's "In Dreams" appearing on the website for *Blue Velvet*'s soundtrack are a bit different: "In dreams you're mine/All of the time with you/Ever in dreams, in dreams."

8. Lynch, *Lynch on Lynch*, p. 231.

9. Eric Bentley, *The Life of the Drama* (New York: Atheneum, 1970), p. 215.

10. "Fraudulent simulations of festivity" is a phrase from "Spectacle," an entry by Jonathan Crary in *New Keywords: A Revised Vocabulary of Culture and Society*, ed. Tony Bennett, Lawrence Grossberg, and Meaghan Morris (Malden, MA: Blackwell, 2005), p. 335.

11. Bentley, *The Life of the Drama*, p. 205.

12. Bentley discusses melodrama as a site of tears and as a channel for "working off emotion" in *The Life of the Drama*, p. 197.

13. Peter Brooks, *The Melodramatic Imagination: Balzac, Henry James, Melodrama, and the Mode of Excess* (New York: Columbia University Press, 1985), p. 204.

14. See Susanne Langer, *Feeling and Form* (New York: Charles Scribner's Sons, 1953) and Colin McGinn, *The Power of Movies: How Screen and Mind Interact* (New York: Pantheon Books, 2005).

15. Lynch, *Lynch on Lynch*, p. 138.

16. Lynch, *Lynch on Lynch*, p. 13.

17. Lynch, *Lynch on Lynch*, p. 17.

18. Lynch, *Lynch on Lynch*, p. 20.

19. Lynch, *Lynch on Lynch*, p. 15.

20. Lynch, *Lynch on Lynch*, p. 18.

21. Lynch, *Lynch on Lynch*, p. 150.

22. Todd Haynes, *Far from Heaven, Safe, Superstar: The Karen Carpenter Story. Three Screenplays* (New York: Grove Press, 2003), p. viii.

23. Haynes, *Far from Heaven*, p. xiii.

24. Haynes, *Far from Heaven*, p. xiv.

25. Haynes, *Far from Heaven*, p. x.

26. Haynes, *Far from Heaven*, p. x.

27. Haynes, *Far from Heaven*, pp. x–xi.

28. Haynes, *Far from Heaven*, p. 19.

29. Haynes, *Far from Heaven*, p. 3.

30. See Langford, *Film Genre*, p. 38.

31. Haynes, *Far from Heaven*, p. x.

32. Quoted in Haynes, *Far from Heaven*, p. xii.

33. Haynes, *Far from Heaven*, p. xii.

4

Tragicomic Accidents

As it mixes genres, styles, and moods, often in a wayward manner, hybrid cinema flirts with chance and chaos, defying critics and artists who for centuries advocated a contrary aesthetic stemming from Aristotle's *Poetics*: works of art should include only what is likely and necessary, and the incidents in a drama (particularly in a tragedy) should arise "because of one another," rather than through "chance or fortune."[1] Such stress on necessity, logic, and causality has been challenged increasingly—in theatrical and other arts as well as in film—as false to life, which art is supposed to mirror, and to the creative process. One challenge was voiced by Susan Sontag amid the artistic and cultural ferment of the 1960s:

> Ever since the enterprise of criticism began with Aristotle's *Poetics* critics have been beguiled into emphasizing the necessary in art. . . . Usually critics who want to praise a work of art feel compelled to demonstrate that each part is justified, that it could not be other than it is. And every artist, when it comes to his own work, remembering the role of chance, fatigue, external distractions, knows what the critic says to be a lie, knows that it could well have been otherwise. The sense of inevitability that a great work of art projects is not made up of the inevitability or necessity of its parts, but of the whole.[2]

The notion that occurrences of chance and accident in art and artistic practice need not betoken fault or failure was hardly new in the 1960s, nearly a half century after the advent of Dada, and then of Surrealism. Moreover, Sontag's challenge came in the wake of further artistic developments, including Happenings, the Theatre of the Absurd, and the works of Cage and Cunningham, which contested the authority of logic and necessity, while elevating the role of chance and randomness.

THE ROLE OF CHANCE IN FILM

Promoters of mainstream films since cinema's earliest days have cited the importance of necessity; in praising *The Great Train Robbery*, for instance, a publicity catalog of 1904 stated that ". . . every foot must be an essential part, whose loss would deprive the story of some merit; there should be sequence, each part leading to the next with increasing interest. . . ."[3] Moreover, comparable standards were applied to other arts, so that critics decried Arnold Schoenberg's musical compositions, for example, as "strung together at random,"[4] and dismissed paintings by Picasso and Cézanne exhibited at the 1913 Armory Show in New York as "hysteria made visible."[5] Yet enthusiastic reactions to the first short documentaries produced by the Lumières and the Edison Studio in the 1890s were due in part to the natural, spontaneous air of these films, to their openness to chance, accident, and the uncontrollable events of everyday life. Indeed, decades after these first documentaries appeared, Siegfried Kracauer observed that given the abundance of photographic data in just about *every* motion picture, even fiction films shot inside a studio were bound to contain accidents—information unintended or unnoticed by the filmmakers, but capable of surprising and instructing alert spectators.[6] Perhaps such was Ross McElwee's finding, as I wrote in the chapter "Fact and Fiction," when he studied Patricia Neal and Gary Cooper in the fiction film, *Bright Leaf.*

Kracauer is but one of a host of critics, theorists, and filmmakers, including André Bazin and Cesare Zavattini, who have regarded film as predominately a photographic medium deployed most appropriately to reproduce and reveal physical reality and real-life events, including random, accidental occurrences. According to these commentators, however, the narrative and ideological thrust of most motion pictures obscures rather than illuminates reality. While most films stress logical, causal connections between events, writes Bazin, "true cinema gives primacy to succession over causality"[7] and films best unfold "on the level of pure accident."[8] Hence Bazin underscores the validity in the cinema of random, spontaneous events, which—unlike those in Eisenstein's *October* (1927–28), for instance—are "subservient" neither to a "general dramatic direction" nor to an ideology.[9] Zavattini, who scripted major Italian Neorealist films such as *Bicycle Thief* (1948) and *Umberto D* (1951), possibly went further in rejecting firm dramatic and ideological frameworks, as when he called for films in which little if anything happens: just "sit Peter or Paul on a chair," he said, and let them "tell the truth about themselves."[10] Similarly, Michelangelo Antonioni, in directing *L'Avventura* (1960), disavowed "logical narrative transitions," and insisted that cinema "be tied to the truth rather than logic."[11]

Yet another sort of realist perspective has been invoked to justify chance and accident rather than logic and necessity in the cinema. This alternative perspective considers film an ideal medium for revealing and reproducing mental life, rather than either physical or social reality. French novelist Alain Robbe-Grillet, who wrote the screenplay for *Last Year at Marienbad*, directed by Alain Resnais, stated, ". . . I saw Resnais's work as an attempt to construct a purely mental space and time—those of dreams, perhaps, or of memory, those of any affective life—without worrying too much about the traditional relations of cause and effect, or about the absolute time sequence in the narrative."[12] Thus *Last Year at Marienbad* eschews, says Robbe-Grillet, commercial cinema's linear plots and "'logical' developments."[13] Instead, *Marienbad* represents "the total cinema of our mind," which "admits both in alternation and to the same degree . . . present fragments of reality proposed by sight and hearing, and past fragments, or future fragments, or fragments that are completely phantasmagoric."[14] Here then, says Robbe-Grillet, is a cinema of "pure subjectivities," relating a story that "will seem the most realistic, the truest, the one that best corresponds to [the spectator's] . . . emotional life, as soon as [the spectator] . . . agrees to abandon ready-made ideas. . . ."[15]

Of course, cinematic thought and practice had long anticipated Robbe-Grillet's focus on film's affinity to mental life rather than to the external physical world. In the silent era, for example, not only Dadaist and Surrealist films trafficked in "phantasmagoric" sequences and fragments of "pure subjectivities," but also films that departed less radically from narrative logic and linearity, such as works by Méliès, Griffith's *Intolerance*, and *The Cabinet of Dr. Caligari* (1919, Robert Weine). Further, in 1916, the year *Intolerance* appeared, theorist Hugo Münsterberg in *The Film: A Psychological Study* proposed as

Robbe-Grillet would that film bears greater affinity to mental and emotional life than to external reality. Münsterberg wrote, in italics, that *the photoplay tells us the human story by overcoming the forms of the outer world, namely, space, time, and causality. . . .*"[16] "Our mind is here and there," he added, "our mind turns to the present and then to the past: the photoplay [which cuts freely from one place, time, and physical action to another] can equal it in its freedom from the bondage of the material world."[17] He also noted that human "imagination anticipates the future or overcomes reality by fancies and dreams; the photoplay [does] . . . all this more richly than any chance imagination would succeed in doing."[18] However, perhaps more concerned than Robbe-Grillet that motion pictures, in mirroring the random turns of mental and emotional life, not devolve into chaos, Münsterberg called for cinematic art to observe Aristotle's strictures about unity of action and necessity. In a film, wrote the German-born psychologist, ". . . nothing has the right to existence which is not internally needed for the unfolding of the unified action."[19]

Creators of recent hybrid cinema in the United States, which combines genres, styles, images, and moods in amusing as well as jarring ways, usually avoid the gravity of both schools of realism I have described, as well as Münsterberg's stringent call for unity and necessity. Nonetheless, the U.S. filmmakers tend to be drawn to one school of realism or the other. Probably the dream-likeness of David Lynch's films attests to film's affinities to inner life, for example. By contrast, the splinter caught in Vig's hand in *Three Kings*, causing him to cry out as he and his friends attack an enemy fortress, reflects writer-director David O. Russell's determination to stress the importance of mundane, physical accidents within the epic framework of a war movie.[20]

Quentin Tarantino also relates chance and accident, which of course can be less trivial than a splinter, to a central vocation of hybrid cinema when he states, as noted in this book's introduction, "The idea is to take genre characters and put them in real-life situations and make them live by real-life rules. In normal movies, they're too busy telling the plot to have guns go off accidentally and kill someone we don't give a damn about. But it happens. . . ."[21] Thus in Tarantino's view, revealing or invoking real life is important both for its own sake and as a way to disrupt and subvert genres. He has also remarked on "the way violence plays out in your life, all of a sudden. Very rarely does violence build up in real life the way it does in movies. It explodes in your face."[22] Presumably Tarantino's films portray violence accurately; even more important, though, is the compatibility of his view of real-life violence and his endorsement of hybrid cinema's preference for unexpected shifts of style, genre, action, and mood. Just as violence "explodes" in real life, musical sequences in Godard's films and Captain Koons's visit to Butch's childhood home in *Pulp Fiction* come "out of nowhere."[23]

If hybrid cinema's play with genre and style is its top priority, while rendering physical reality and real-life events is subsidiary, the import of inner life is constant. Particularly in works like David Lynch's *Blue Velvet* and *Mulholland Drive*, as I have suggested, hybrid form seems inextricable from radical turns in the mental and emotional lives of the film's characters. Even when the content is not subjective as in Lynch's films, moreover, hybrid cinema's incessant play with form reflects an overarching consciousness, whether individual or collective, directing events on the screen. Unlike style in realist cinema as discussed by Bazin, Zavattini, and Kracauer, and unlike classical Hollywood style in the 1930s and '40s, style in hybrid cinema is rarely invisible. The spectator is kept keenly aware—as the hybrid film shifts generic gear, or as it abruptly alters color, light, texture, or focus—that what Münsterberg termed the "light flitting immateriality"[24] on the screen is not identical to the natural world; nor is it merely a technological occurrence. Rather, hybrid form is above all a human fabrication, a projection of human thought and feeling, often brimming with references to prior acts of imagination in film, television, music, theatre, painting, and so on.

By way of summary, then, abrupt shifts and aberrations that come "out of nowhere" in hybrid cinema, whether like turns of mental and emotional life or changes in physical reality, often seem arbitrary and accidental instead of rational and necessary. Hence hybrid cinema reflects the rising, complex interest in chance evinced in film and other arts over the past hundred years. Such cinema also portrays a world that feels as unstable and unpredictable as the one we live in. Like our world, hybrid cinema spins out of control, or threatens to do so, yielding results that are both tragic and farcical. Perhaps the most powerful intersections of accident, tragedy, and comedy appear not in recent hybrid films, however, but in earlier ones such as *Rules of the Game* (1939, Jean Renoir), *Monsieur Verdoux* (1947, Charles Chaplin), *Dr. Strangelove. Or How I Learned to Stop Worrying and Love the Bomb* (1964, Stanley Kubrick), and *Nashville* (1975, Robert Altman). These masterworks prefigure recent hybrid cinema's focus on tragicomic accidents.

Rules of the Game

At the end of Renoir's seemingly comic *Rules of the Game*, in which skittish aristocrats and their servants compete for status and love at their chateau getaway, The Marquis, Robert de la Chesnaye (Marcel Dalio), makes the following somber announcement to his guests after André Jurieu (Roland Toutain), trans-Atlantic aviator and hero, has been fatally shot in the night by Schumacher (Gaston Modot), Robert's gamekeeper: "Gentlemen, there has just been a deplorable accident, that's all. . . . My keeper Schumacher thought he saw a poacher, and he fired, since that is his duty. . . . Chance had it that André Jurieu should be the victim of this error. . . ." Whereupon the savvy aristocrat Saint-Aubin (Pierre Nay), standing at the base of the stairway below Robert, scoffs to a fellow guest, "A new definition of the word ACCIDENT!"

Schumacher did not really think Jurieu was a poacher of rabbits. Rather, he mistook him for Jurieu's friend, Octave (Jean Renoir), whom Schumacher thought he saw in the garden passionately kissing Lisette (Paulette Dubost), Schumacher's wife. But rather than Lisette, employed as Christine's maid, Octave was kissing Christine (Nora Grégor), Robert's wife, who at Lisette's urging was wearing Lisette's cloak in the chilly night. Octave was preparing to run off with Christine, not with Lisette, until Lisette, as he returned from the garden to retrieve his coat, objected that he was too old and poor to make Christine happy. Consequently Octave, mindful of Jurieu's passion for Christine, urged the hero to replace him. Surrendering his warm coat to Jurieu, he told him to meet Christine at the green-house and take her away as Octave had hoped to do.

Earlier in the evening, amid theatrical entertainments organized by the Marquis that failed to restrain the antic passions of the aristocrats and their employees, Schumacher chased and fired his gun at the lowly rabbit-poacher Marceau (Julien Carette) for daring to woo Lisette. Finally the mayhem led Robert, who until recently was cheating on Christine as she perhaps cheated on him, to demand that his majordomo, Corneille (Eddy Debray), "Get this comedy stopped!" (Or, "Stop this farce!").

The slaying of Jurieu was and was not an accident, then. And the comedy or farce had to end tragically because the main characters' passions and deceits were out of control. The film implies, moreover, that in turning the chateau into a jungle, its characters behaved no differently than French society beyond the chateau's gates. Hence this famous exchange between Octave and Christine after she becomes aware of Robert's adultery for three years with Geneviève de Marrast (Mila Parely):

> Christine: For three years my life has been based on a lie. I haven't been able to think of anything else since I saw them together at the hunt, and suddenly realized.

> Octave: Listen, Christine, that's a sign of the times too. We're in a period when everyone tells lies: pharmacists' handbills, Governments, the radio, the cinema, the newspapers. . . . So how could you expect us poor individuals not to lie as well?

Perhaps Octave states merely the obvious—as true of the world today as it was then. In any case, the French government banned *Rules of the Game* and its depiction of a nation devoid of integrity on the eve of World War II.

Monsieur Verdoux

"What a relief to get away from the jungle fight," an increasingly grave and fatigued Henri Verdoux (Charles Chaplin) tells his wife Mona (Mady Correll) upon arriving home one afternoon to join her for their tenth wedding anniversary. The following morning he will once again leave her and their young son Peter to return to the fight: marrying and killing rich women for their money. Termed by Chaplin "a comedy of murders," *Monsieur Verdoux* offers a range of comic styles, including slapstick, which arises early in the film with the spattering of food and drink in the home of the Couvais family, one of whose female members has disappeared—a victim of Verdoux. But in addition to comedy, *Monsieur Verdoux* obviously sounds tragic notes. Not only do innocent women die, but an intelligent, sensitive, and witty man, once a hardworking citizen and still a loving husband and father, turns late in life into a killing machine. A bit like Chaplin's Tramp as viewed by Andrew Sarris, Chaplin's Verdoux is "precariously balanced between the domains of comedy and tragedy."[25]

Much the same can be said of Chaplin's dual persona in *The Great Dictator* (1940), which appeared one year after *Rules of the Game*. Daring to mock Hitler's regime as few if any in Hollywood had, Chaplin in *The Great Dictator* plays two tragicomic characters: Hynkel, the volatile dictator who dances coquettishly with a balloon globe when he is not emitting genocidal gibberish;

and the barber, an everyman struggling to stay clear of Hynkel who finds himself mistaken for him. Chaplin's shifts of mood and manner in *The Great Dictator* often seem driven simply by his shifts from one character to the other. But in *Monsieur Verdoux* Chaplin enacts extreme shifts of tone as one hybrid character, the bluebeard Verdoux. This man of many parts is sufficiently complex to be shocked not only by global crises such as the Depression of the 1930s and the rise of European Fascism, but also by sharp changes in his own spirit and conduct. Reflecting on his murderous career after it is over, Verdoux stands like a stranger outside himself, momentarily aghast at his deeds, at the person he has become, regarding his villainy as a nightmare from which he has at last awakened. Although shaken by such reflections, he nevertheless steps impenitently from his prison cell to his execution, relieved to be leaving a world in which the business of mass murder on a far vaster scale than he transacted has become the norm. "Wars, conflict, it's all business," he tells the judge and jury before his execution. "One murder makes a villain; millions a hero. Numbers sanctify."

Unlike *Rules of the Game*, *Monsieur Verdoux* does not specifically speak of accident. The term does not arise as a euphemism for murder, for instance, or as a way of identifying origins or results of tragicomic situations. Yet accident figures as centrally in Chaplin's film as death does. We are told, for instance, that Verdoux suddenly lost his job as a bank teller after thirty years because of the Depression, but we are not given the reason he was the first to go despite his seniority. Nor does the film inquire into the causes of the Depression—or of business villainy, sudden declines in stock prices, or the ascent of Hitler and Mussolini. Such interrelated events seem in the film arbitrary and mysterious, perhaps as they seemed to millions of people who actually lived through them. Hence such events function in *Monsieur Verdoux* as "deplorable accidents" (as Robert de la Chesnaye might say)—dire happenings that lack clear causes and defy most means of rational address.

Dr. Strangelove

In *Dr. Strangelove. Or How I Learned to Stop Worrying and Love the Bomb*, accident again proves significant, as it obliges U.S. President Merkin Muffley (Peter Sellers) to disclose secret data to USSR Premier Dimitri Kissoff that will enable his armed forces to destroy U.S. warplanes mistakenly on their way to bomb his country with nuclear weapons. "How the hell could the President ever tell the Russian Premier to shoot down American planes? Good Lord, it sounds ridiculous," mused Stanley Kubrick as he prepared the treatment for the film; but he considered the alternative to President Muffley's action equally ludicrous: "After all," he said, "what could be more absurd than the very idea of two megapowers willing to wipe out all human life because of an accident. . . ."[26]

Muffley explains to Kissoff on the "hotline" that a U.S. general, "one of our base commanders, he had a sort of—well, he went a little funny in the head. You know, just a little *funny*. And, uh, he went and did a silly thing . . . he ordered his planes . . . to attack your country." The President's descriptions—"a little funny in the head," "did a silly thing"—perhaps befit quaint characters in screwball comedies of the 1930s such as *Mr. Deeds Goes to Town* (1938, Frank Capra) more than General Jack Ripper (Sterling Hayden), the would-be mass killer who has unleashed the bombers. Kissoff's ambassador in Washington, summoned by Muffley to the U.S. War Room to help the President and his advisers stop the bombers and avert nuclear war, warns that it may be too late. The Soviets' hitherto secret Doomsday machine, he explains, will explode automatically, and likely destroy the whole planet, if but one U.S. plane gets through. Hence Muffley's amiable description of Ripper and of what the general has done seems even more off the mark than before. Yet the President's words point to a crucial way in which tragedy and comedy converge in this saga. Not just ordinary language, but also habits of thought, emotion, and conduct prove wildly inadequate in addressing truths of war, especially in the nuclear age.

Probably Muffley behaves more sensibly than most characters do. By contrast, Major T. J. "King" Kong (Slim Pickens), who commands one of the attacking planes, responds to the attack order by donning a cowboy hat, which he waves ecstatically at film's end, as he rides—as he might a wild bronco at a rodeo—a bomb labeled "Hi There!" into the icy Soviet wasteland below. Back in the War Room, Dr. Strangelove (Sellers again), a German-born scientist with a metallic hand, like *Metropolis*'s Rotwang (1927, Fritz Lang), reverts to a prior allegiance after telling President Muffley that the United States could recover from nuclear war by stowing its most gifted citizens—about ten women to each man—in mine shafts or underground sanctuaries, there to copulate and reproduce for as long as it takes. Evidently invigorated by these prospects, Strangelove rises miraculously from his wheelchair, and shouts, as he totters and trembles, "Mein Führer—I can walk!" Then, over images of nuclear explosions and mushroom clouds, a romantic ditty is audible—"We'll meet again. Don't know where. Don't know when." Similarly, "Try a little tenderness," another sweet tune, succeeded the report at the film's outset of Soviet development in the Arctic waste of "the ultimate weapon, a doomsday device." Just as the film's psychotic characters react bizarrely to events, *Dr. Strangelove* itself, like *The Atomic Café*, is rife with incongruities of mood and image that render humankind's destruction chillingly funny.

Nashville

The coquettish disconnect between the doomsday plan and "Try a little tenderness," and between that plan's explosive consequences and "We'll meet again," prefigures the counterpoint at the end of *Nashville* between the shooting of country and western star Barbara Jean (Ronee Blakley), as she performs at the outdoor concert space called the Parthenon, and the defiant song that immediately follows her being carried from the stage: "You may say that I ain't free/But it don't worry me." Shaken by the shooting but briefly, the audience remains in place, and soon joins the unknown singer Albuquerque (Barbara Harris), who has been loitering on the edge of the film's action thirsting for stardom, in her hymn to indifference and to the denial of reality (Is it really possible to be free of worry when one is not free?). As puzzling as the song and the crowd's response is why another fringe character, Kenny Fraiser (David Hayward), whose purposes have been murkier than Albuquerque's, shoots Barbara Jean, the beloved star whose emotional state has been one of perpetual nervous collapse. Unclear too is why Kenny acts at the Parthenon, appropriated for the day by a third-party U.S. Presidential campaign, and in the city of Nashville, hailed by Haven Hamilton (Henry Gibson), Barbara Jean's canny country and western ally, as the Athens of the South.

Robert Altman said he intended *Nashville* as a "metaphor for America,"[27] though viewers would be inclined to investigate the broader society his film reflects even without his suggestion. Kenny Fraiser's unexplained deed seems reasonless and arbitrary—and in this sense accidental. Yet he acts deliberately, in a metaphorically murderous environment where feverish competition for fame and power contributes to Barbara Jean's illness, and stifles prospects for a happier, more peaceful community. If *Nashville*'s numerous characters appear on screen and relate to one another "by apparent accident," as one critic has indicated,[28] the reason may be that selfish, brutish people, as Thomas Hobbes once suggested, exist in chaos.

Certainly *Nashville* reflects a society in which raw violence is growing more commonplace—as indicated, for example, by the insouciant reaction when multiple vehicles crash on the freeway early in the film (after Barbara Jean's arrival at the airport), in a reprise of the endless traffic jam and the wreckage with its bloody deaths in Godard's *Weekend*. There is also Lady Pearl's (Barbara Baxley) unappeasable grief over President John Kennedy's assassination, plus the dialogue about assassination between Opal (Geraldine Chaplin), the British reporter, and political operative John Triplette (Michael Murphy), who sets up the concert where Barbara Jean is shot. Somewhat like *Rules of the Game* and *Dr. Strangelove*, then, *Nashville* reflects a society propelled by competition and aggression, with citizens increasingly disconnected from one another and from themselves, as well as from any reality beyond their own constricted social and political clime. In this tense, airless environment, destructive "accidents" are waiting to happen, and waiting to transform comedy and farce into tragedy. The strong likelihood of such accidents occurring in films like *Rules*, *Strangelove*, and *Nashville* brings to mind Fred Astaire's contention in *Shall We Dance?* (1937, Mark Sandrich) that "chance is the fool's name for fate."

ACCIDENT AS THE FULCRUM OF TRAGICOMIC SEQUENCES

The shifts of mood, style, and genre in recent hybrid films that often seem whimsical or arbitrary lend these films an aleatoric air. In addition, "accident" occasionally serves as the explicit fulcrum of tragicomic sequences in these films. An example is the scene in the car in *Pulp Fiction* in which Vincent shoots Marvin, one of the young hoods who failed to level with Vincent's boss Marsellus. "I just accidentally shot Marvin in the throat," Vincent tells Jules, who responds by seeking a cause or reason: "Why the fuck did you do that?" Vincent replies it was an accident precisely because he had no reason or intention to shoot Marvin: "I didn't mean to do it. I said it was an accident." Then:

Jules: I've seen a lot of crazy-ass shit in my time—

Vincent: —chill out, man, it was an accident, okay? You probably hit a bump or somethin' and the gun went off.

Jules: The car didn't hit no motherfuckin' bump!

Vincent: Look! I didn't mean to shoot this son-of-a-bitch, the gun just went off, don't ask me how!

Here as elsewhere in the film, the two criminals evince little sympathy for their victims, which perhaps makes the situation comic as well as gruesome. In particular, Vincent's almost nonchalant response to the death renders it less real, somewhat like death and physical injury in cartoons, Mack Sennett comedies, and perhaps *Dr. Strangelove.* The sense of unreality may enable the film's spectator to feel momentarily relieved and carefree, rather than aghast at the killing, or guilty for enjoying it. Yet a different sidestepping of death is performed by Jules. Certainly he is more troubled by the killing than Vincent is, and more troubled than when he himself fatally shot Marvin's cohort, Brett. But what disturbs Jules more than the destruction of a young life is the lack of satisfactory explanation for it. Jules is distracted from his quest for an explanation, though, by the urgent need to evade the police, dispose of Marvin's body, and cleanse himself, Vincent, and the car's interior of Marvin's spattered remains.

The tension between Jules and Vincent over the lack of explanation for Marvin's death immediately succeeds another dispute in which they argue a bit more abstractly over the role of causality in human affairs. Jules insists that events have how's and why's; Vincent argues that some things just happen—inexplicably. The dispute first arises when, as Jules and Vincent threaten Marvin and his gang in their apartment, a gang member "tightly clutching his huge silver .357 Magnum,"[29] bursts out of hiding in the bathroom and fires "six booming shots"[30] close range at Jules and Vincent. When not one of the bullets hits either man, Vincent chalks their survival up to good fortune, whereas Jules attributes it to divine intervention:

Jules: We should be fuckin' dead!

Vincent: Yeah, we were lucky.

Jules: That shit wasn't luck. That shit was somethin' else.

Vincent: Yeah, maybe.

Jules: That was ... divine intervention. You know what divine intervention is?

Vincent: Yeah, I think so. That means God came down from Heaven and stopped the bullets.

Jules: Yeah, man, that's what it means. That's exactly what it means! God came down from Heaven and stopped the bullets.

Observing that Vincent remains unconvinced that God intervened, Jules warns him not to "blow this shit off"; then, when Vincent stubbornly maintains, ". . . this shit happens," Jules retorts, "Wrong, wrong, this shit doesn't just happen."

In the next scene in a car as Jules and Vincent drive off with their captive Marvin in the back seat, Vincent cites an episode from the TV series *Cops* to support his claim that things *do* just happen. A cop "unloads on this guy," says Vincent, "and doesn't hit nothin'. And these guys were in a hallway. It's a freak, but it happens." Again disturbed by what he regards as Vincent's callow view, Jules declares that he means to leave his criminal life and take up the service of God: "From here on in, you can consider my ass retired." Taken aback, Vincent solicits Marvin's opinion as to how and why the six booming shots from the Magnum missed both Jules and Vincent. When Marvin responds that he has no opinion, Vincent prods him: "C'mon, Marvin. You gotta have an opinion. Do you think God came down from Heaven and stopped the bullets?" But before Marvin can reply, Vincent's gun goes off, killing him and prompting yet more debate between Jules and Vincent as to whether events must have causes and purposes.

Their stubborn disagreement recapitulates a tension central to hybrid cinema, in which both form and content often hinge on encounters between random and deliberate events, between chance and design. Indeed, what might be called technical effects in hybrid cinema often raise issues of chance and design simultaneously. As discussed in the chapter on hybrid documentaries, for instance, elliptical editing and abrupt shifts of color, grain, focus, light, motion, and camera position in *Mr. Death: The Rise and Fall of Fred A. Leuchter, Jr.* can at first seem arbitrary. But these shifts ultimately constitute a unique pattern, mood, or world evidencing the filmmaker's deliberateness. Further, while these technical effects initially seem but ironic tics, glitches, or accidents, they eventually point—or so I argue in the documentary chapter—to new avenues of feeling and meaning.

Yet another familiar tension in hybrid cinema reflected in the dispute between Jules and Vincent concerns the divide between hot and cool responses to events. Jules warns Vincent not to coldly "blow this shit off," because Jules himself can no longer blow it off. Jules suddenly perceives more purpose and promise in the world, and finds himself morally engaged as never before. Vincent remains detached, however, with no dawning vision of any grand narrative or purpose in life, a man of perhaps trivial material interests who accepts far more coolly than Jules the possibility that life comes down to chance and accident—or that life is a "series of unrelated actions" as posited in Albert Camus's *The Myth of Sisyphus*.[31] Unlike the French intellectual, though, Vincent shrugs off humankind's incapacity to understand the universe or to set it in order. Possibly he represents, then, hybrid cinema's flippant side, as well as its skepticism toward conventions of form and feeling, and its comfort with anarchy and formlessness; whereas Jules in his spiritual conversion brings to mind this cinema's strong, contrary attraction to design, purpose, and moral action.

Like Vincent, Jules remains a comical figure, even after his conversion, which occurs in a post-religious era and draws nearly as much inspiration from popular television as from the Bible. Further, both men enjoy comedy's blessing in that they evade death, the gangster's standard fate. But it is primarily Jules, with his hope in a higher order, in grand purposes, who espies suffering and tragedy as well as redemption; Vincent, for his part, is content to travel light and take his chances.

Slacker

Camus's phrase, "series of unrelated actions," appears in a passage Richard Linklater cites at the end of the published script of *Slacker* (1991), his influential, independent fiction film that looks and sounds much like a documentary, and that proceeds without a central character or plot through a series of seemingly unrelated incidents. At the start, a young man (Linklater), arriving by bus in Austin, Texas, early in the morning, takes a taxi and delivers a monologue to the driver (Rudy Basquez) about a dream he has had on the bus—one of those "completely real" dreams, he explains, that, according to the book he was reading in the dream, provide glimpses into other realities. The young man, identified in the script as "Should Have Stayed at Bus Station," anticipates the preoccupation—in Linklater's *Waking Life* (2001) as well as in *Slacker*—with both the unpredictable dream-likeness of our lives and the belief that our random thoughts and dreams create or represent other realities, which in fact exist alongside our own. Should Have Stayed at Bus Station adds that we ordinarily fail to see these "separate realities," or parallel universes, "because we're kind of trapped in this one reality restriction type of thing." His talk of multiple realities sets the stage for the diverse outlooks and activities of the "slackers" who succeed him in this film. Further, his talk may remind the spectator that diverse cinematic outlooks and activities, perhaps ordinarily separated from one another, merge in hybrid cinema.

After Should Have Stayed at Bus Station gets out of the taxi, he confronts what seems to be a real-life accident rather than a mere thought or dream. A thud is heard as he strolls from the taxi, and the camera pans from him to a station wagon turning right, out of frame. Without a cut, the camera move continues ahead of the young man, roughly in the direction he is walking, to reveal an unconscious woman sprawled on the ground with groceries strewn nearby. In the ongoing long take, Should Have Stayed at Bus Station re-enters the frame in the background and casually steps closer to the camera to stand over the fallen body and inspect it. The camera pulls back, a female jogger (Jan Hockey, called "Jogger" in the script) enters the frame, and, jogging in place, instructs the young man not to touch the body, but to get an ambulance and the police and to contact the victim's family. He takes the victim's pocketbook and walks toward a public phone across the street in the background. A car enters the bottom of the frame and stops; the male driver, "Running Late" (Stephan Hockey), gets out; he asks Jogger what happened. "Accident," she says, "but everything's under control."

But *Slacker* soon raises the possibility that what has been called an accident was in fact deliberate and controlled. Thus, like other films discussed in this chapter, *Slacker* establishes a tension almost immediately between chance and design. Further, like more epic films such as *Nashville* and *Dr. Strangelove*, Linklater's film quickly underscores frailties and improprieties of human feeling that are at once tragic and laughable. Indeed, tragicomic notes abound in this odd film, which commences in an accident that is reframed as matricide.

Following Jogger's assurance that "everything's under control," Running Late ignores the victim and expresses interest instead in Jogger; he hands her his card, suggests she call him, and speeds off. A passerby primarily interested in the victim's groceries, and consequently named "Grocery Grabber" (Sam Dietert), enters the frame and asks whose body lies on the ground. Jogger gives him the card she has just been handed and tells him, ". . . call this guy." She jogs away slowly, nonchalantly. The camera pans screen left to reveal the station wagon from earlier in the shot re-entering and parking, and its young driver emerging. Finally, there is a cut to a new scene. Thus the long take I have just described, beginning with Should Have Stayed at Bus Station walking from the taxi, encompasses in one continuous space five characters, plus the traffic victim. Not one of these characters makes significant contact with another, or seems particularly moved by the fate of the victim. Rather, these five individuals who overlap in space and time share a condition of atomized numbness or indifference.

The driver of the station wagon, identified in the script as "Hit-and-run Son" (Mark James), enters an apartment. Inside he receives a telephone call about the accident; at first he tells the caller that his mother, with whom he apparently lives, has yet to wake up. He seems even more detached about the accident and its victim than were the strangers on the street moments earlier. Hit-and-run Son lights candles on a shrine plastered with religious and other images. Then he cuts pictures from a high school yearbook, and sets them aflame. He picks up a microphone attached to a tape deck; sets the microphone in the open window as police sirens are heard; turns on a film projector, and, as police bang on the apartment door, plays a home movie of a woman pushing and playfully kicking a toy car in which sits a child. Hit-and-run Son abandons this film loop that possibly depicts his earlier life with his mother, opens the apartment door, and, holding a bag he may have prepared in anticipation of his arrest, surrenders to the police, who handcuff him. On the street, one bystander matter-of-factly tells another: ". . . it looks like some guy ran over his mother."

What becomes of Hit-and-run Son, Jogger, Should Have Stayed at Bus Station, and other individuals who appear up to this point is a mystery, since they vanish from the film as it shifts to other characters, concerns, and incidents that happen into the frame. Similarly, the how's and why's of Hit-and-run Son's conduct, and of his relationship with his mother, are left dangling. The film thus supplants conventional narrative logic and continuity with chance and discontinuity as it wanders with mild Surrealist wit and abandon from one reality, or "reality restriction type of thing," to another, surveying a welter of human desires and emotional disconnections.

Broken Flowers

In *Broken Flowers* (2005, Jim Jarmusch), Don Johnston (Bill Murray) sets out by bus, plane, and car to discover which of his many former lovers has written the anonymous letter he has just received suggesting he unknowingly fathered her son about 19 years ago, and that the young man may now be looking for him. The "hypothetical son," as Don refers to him, would be approximately Hit-and-run Son's age; and while the latter seems colder and crueler than Don, there is some resemblance between them. In fact, Don in his emotional minimalism resembles all of the characters who approach the accident victim early in *Slacker*.

Possibly he is not entirely bloodless or unfeeling, though. One reviewer sees "playing across Mr. Murray's mouth and eyes" in *Broken Flowers* "longing, disappointment, bafflement and an earnest sense of wonder."[32] Another reviewer observes, "Ever since Sofia Coppola cast him as the alienated movie star in *Lost in Translation*, Murray has been exploring his regret-in-autumn side to touching, tragicomic effect."[33] In any case, Don does look blank, drained, and passionless much of the time; and when his latest lover Sherry (Julie Delpy, who starred also in Linklater's *Before Sunrise* [1995] and *Before Sunset* [2004]) leaves him at the start of *Broken Flowers*, deriding any claims he may have to

When his latest lover leaves him, Don Johnston (Bill Murray) reveals a "regret-in-autumn side to touching, tragicomic effect," as Carina Chocano writes in the Los Angeles Times. *BAC Films, Focus Features/The Kobal Collection/Lee, David.*

being a Don Juan, he remains fixed on his fine sofa, unable to muster any af-
fect whatever. His demeanor brings to mind Should Have Remained at Bus
Station's comment to the cab driver in *Slacker* that in his vivid, realistic dream
on the bus, ". . . there was nothing going on at all."

It's difficult to feel sorry for Don, perhaps because he refuses to question
his psychological predicament. Moreover, a wealthy, retired computer entrepreneur who now refuses to own a computer, Don has the advantage of every
material comfort, including a svelte home theatre system and an expensive
car. So he is a lot better off than another silent male in search of family, Travis
(Harry Dean Stanton) in *Paris, Texas* (1984, Wim Wenders), who not only
trembles with strong emotions he cannot put into words, but lives in abject
poverty. Unlike Travis, furthermore, Don has left behind, in the words of Carina Chocano in the *Los Angeles Times*, "a trail of dead relationships"[34] ("Dead
Flowers" was the film's working title), which he seems reluctant to acknowledge.

Another obstacle to pitying Don is that his encounters on his journey to
find the letter's author are acutely amusing as well as disappointing. For instance, no "over-the-hill Don Juan," as Sherry called Don, should have to confront the allure of naked Lolita (Alexis Dziena), Laura's (Sharon Stone)
teenage daughter who entertains him until her widowed mother—the first of
a quartet of ex-girlfriends Don visits—arrives home. Although Laura spends
the night with Don, she has no son, nor—in her rundown home and junk-
strewn front yard—a typewriter on which the letter might have been written.
Don gets a decidedly cooler response when he visits prosperous Carmen (Jessica Lange), who now prefers women (like her assistant, Chloë Sevigny) as romantic partners, and who has taken up the career of animal communicator.
The author of such notable books as *Animal and Identity Issues*, Carmen has
little time or inclination, particularly after her cat informs her that Don has a
hidden agenda, to discuss with her old flame either the past or questions
about hypothetical sons. Next, Don finds anxious Dora (Frances Conroy),
who lives with her realtor husband in an antiseptic, prefabricated mansion,
not much more welcoming than Carmen. Finally, Penny (Tilda Swinton), who
lives in a remote retreat for over-the-hill motorcycle gang members, greets
him with, "So what the fuck do you want, Donny?" Don spots a pink typewriter on the ground outside her shack; but when he asks if she has a son, she
replies, "Fuck you, Donny," without exactly explaining why, and lets her Hell's

Angel boyfriend beat Don unconscious and deposit him in his rented car overnight in a sodden field.

After a stop at the gravesite of a fifth ex-girlfriend where the battered Don evinces modest grief, he takes a plane home, and soon meets with Winston (Jeffrey Wright), his Ethiopian friend and neighbor, at a restaurant. Winston arranged Don's trip in the hope Don would solve the mystery of the unbidden letter—and of his long life; but Don, who was hesitant from the outset, now tells his friend, "I think this whole thing is a farce, a fiasco." "Don't worry. We're still going to solve this mystery," says Winston, whereupon Don espies outside the restaurant a young man he also spotted at the airport when he landed. He leaves the restaurant, talks to the youngster, learns he enjoys travel and philosophy, buys him a cheese sandwich, talks some more, and finally says, "I know you think I'm your father, right?" In response the young man re-peats Penny's invective and runs away. Don runs after him, then gives up, and the camera circles Don's still, bereft figure. Like the other episodes in his jour-ney, this chance encounter with the youth yields no solution to the mystery of the letter that arrived out of the blue, or to the puzzle of Don's emotional na-ture and the tragicomic accidents of his life.

NOTES

1. Kenneth A. Telford, *Aristotle's Poetics: Translation and Analysis* (Chicago: Henry Regenery Company, 1961), p. 19.

2. Susan Sontag, *Against Interpretation* (New York: Delta, 1966), p. 33.

3. Quoted in George C. Pratt, *Spellbound in Darkness. A History of Silent Film* (Greenwich, CT: New York Graphic Society Ltd., 1973), p. 37; from "About Moving Picture Films," *Complete Illustrated Catalog of Moving Picture Films, Stereopticons, Slides, Films*, Kleine Optical Company, Chicago, Illinois, October 1904, p. 31.

4. Quoted in Pratt, *Spellbound in Darkness*, p.105; from foreign dispatches to the *Musical Courier* of November 1912.

5. Quoted in Pratt, *Spellbound in Darkness*, p. 106; from the *Atlantic Monthly* of April 1915.

6. See two books by Siegfried Kracauer: *From Caligari to Hitler. A Psychological History of the German Film* (Princeton, NJ: Princeton University Press, 1947) and *Theory of Film. The Redemption of Physical Reality* (New York: Oxford University Press, 1960).

7. André Bazin, *What Is Cinema? Vol. II*, trans. Hugh Gray (Berkeley: University of California Press, 1971), p. 58.

8. Bazin, *What Is Cinema?* p. 59.

9. Bazin, *What Is Cinema?* p. 81.

10. Quoted in Roy Armes, *Patterns of Realism* (New York: A.S. Barnes & Co., 1971), p. 172.

11. Quoted in Ian Cameron and Robin Wood, *Antonioni* (New York: Praeger, 1968), p. 9.

12. Alain Robbe-Grillet, *Last Year at Marienbad*, trans. Richard Howard (New York: Grove Press, 1962), pp. 8–9.

13. Robbe-Grillet, *Last Year at Marienbad*, p. 10.

14. Robbe-Grillet, *Last Year at Marienbad*, p. 13.

15. Robbe-Grillet, *Last Year at Marienbad*, p. 14.

16. Hugo Münsterberg, "Excerpt from *The Film: A Psychological Study*," in Leo Braudy and Marshall Cohen (eds.), *Film Theory and Criticism. Introductory Readings*, Fifth Edition (New York: Oxford University Press, 1999), p. 402.

17. Münsterberg, "Excerpt from *The Film*," p. 405.

18. Münsterberg, "Excerpt from *The Film*," p. 402.

19. Münsterberg, "Excerpt from *The Film*," p. 406.

20. Russell describes his intentions in his commentary on the DVD of *Three Kings*.

21. Quoted in Manohla Dargis, "Quentin Tarantino on *Pulp Fiction*," in Jim Hillier (ed.), *American Independent Cinema* (London: British Film Institute, 2001), pp. 244–45.

22. Quoted in Erik Bauer, "The Mouth and the Method," in Jim Hillier (ed.), *American Independent Cinema*, p. 257.

23. Tarantino told Manohla Dargis, "My favorite musical sequences have always been in Godard, because they just come out of nowhere." See Dargis, "Quentin Tarantino on *Pulp Fiction*," p. 242.

24. Münsterberg, "Excerpt from *The Film*," p. 404.

25. Andrew Sarris, *YOU AIN'T HEARD NOTHIN' YET. The American Talking Film. History and Memory 1927–1949* (New York: Oxford University Press, 1998), p. 149.

26. Quoted in Norman Kagan, *The Cinema of Stanley Kubrick* (New York: Grove Press, 1972), p. 111.

27. Quoted in Robert Kolker, *A Cinema of Loneliness*, Third Edition (New York: Oxford University Press, 2000), p. 375.

28. Kolker, *A Cinema of Loneliness,*, p. 376.

29. Quentin Tarantino, *Pulp Fiction. A Quentin Tarantino Screenplay* (New York: Miramax, 1994), p. 136.

30. Tarantino, *Pulp Fiction*, p. 137.

31. Quoted in Richard Linklater, *Slacker* (New York: St. Martin's Press, 1992), p. 115.

32. A. O. Scott, review of *Broken Flowers, New York Times*, August 5, 2005.

33. Carina Chocano, review of *Broken Flowers, Los Angeles Times*, August 5, 2005.

34. Chocano, review of *Broken Flowers*.

5

Global Parallels

Signaling the global reach of hybrid form in recent years have been numerous foreign films that have enjoyed critical and often commercial success in the United States and abroad. Pedro Almodóvar's cinema of mixed genres, styles, and moods, for instance, has been embraced in the United States and his native Spain as well as around the world. Hybrid qualities also distinguish Stephen Chow's martial arts parodies and other popular Hong Kong cinema, plus the unusual Chinese backstage musical, *The World* (2004, Jia Zhang-ke). Germany too has contributed to hybrid explorations—in films such as *Run Lola Run* (1998), which combines aspects of art cinema with allusions to traditional last-minute rescues and interactive cyber-narratives; subsequent work by writer-director Tom Tykwer, who also composes music for his films, has included *The Princess and the Warrior* (2001), a slower-paced but no less intense hybrid thriller.

The impulses and perceptions underlying recent foreign hybrid cinema derive from ones that have underpinned hybrid ventures in art and film in the United States and abroad throughout film history. The notion of a chance encounter between a sewing machine and an umbrella on a dissecting table, after all, nicely jolts human thought and feeling everywhere from time to time. Like much of hybrid cinema, this Surrealist image epitomizes convergences of sense and nonsense, the ordinary and extraordinary, the real and imaginary, reason and the unconscious—in short, convergences of seemingly distinct and contrary realms of being that are more intertwined than many of us readily admit. Whether such odd juxtapositions in hybrid cinema evoke Surrealism or another artistic movement, they have the capacity to expand truth, pleasure, and freedom. Rarely are film genres as uniform or homogeneous as some definitions imply. Thomas Elsaesser properly underscores the hybrid quality of melodrama when he points to "its shifts in mood, its different tempi, and the mixing of stylistic levels."[1] Moreover, diversity lies in the beholder—in the critic or analyst—as well as in the object or artwork. "Difference and ex-centricity replace homogeneity and centrality as the foci of postmodern social analysis," observes Linda Hutcheon in *The Politics of Postmodernism*.[2] Stirred by perspectives such as Elsaesser's and Hutcheon's, as well as by ones related to Surrealism and other artistic movements, spectators and filmmakers have been drawn increasingly in recent years to departures from homogeneity that result when genres are interrupted and diverted in individual films, or when diverse generic currents clash or swirl together.

Such generic mixing perhaps parallels Raymond Deagan's goal in *Far from Heaven*, shared for a time by Cathy Whitaker, to reach beyond the borders of one's ordinary existence so as to mingle with strangers in unfamiliar environments. Yet another parallel appears in *Pulp Fiction*'s Jules Winnfield as he seeks to transform his experience by identifying more freely and explicitly than he has earlier in life with disparate Biblical characters. Jonathan Caouette in *Tarnation*, and Gates, Barlow, Elgin, and Vig in *Three Kings*, also push beyond restrictive borders of association.

PLURALISM AND POPULAR CINEMA

In both form and content, the hybrid films from around the world discussed in this chapter stress connection as well as difference. At least implicitly, they incline toward wider, more pluralistic experiences, comparable to those in the American films just mentioned. This disposition to reach out may be less than universal at the present historical moment as many social, cultural, and political communities strive to either retain or restore tighter, purer, more contained ways of life. Yet the worth of recent foreign hybrid films, as of many comparable American films, does not depend on their explicit social and political agendas. These films are not moralistic or didactic. They do not score ideological points in the manner of often-dazzling hybrid works such as *Three Kings*, Eisenstein's *Strike*, or films by Godard, Oshima, and Littín in the late

1960s. Decidedly less pontifical than these earlier works, they more closely resemble films like *Fargo, Blue Velvet, Pulp Fiction,* and *Kill Bill.* Contemporary
hybrid films from abroad focus primarily on the immense variety of film history and film language, and on the fluidity of human consciousness, identity,
and possibility. Further, while scarcely anti-intellectual, they are immersed in
popular as well as high culture, and openly smitten by the verve of mass entertainment.

Indeed, popular hybrid films from abroad such as Chow's *Shaolin Soccer*
(2002), the "top-grossing action comedy in Hong Kong history,"[3] and *Kung Fu
Hustle* (2005), the top grossing foreign film in the United States in 2005,[4] in-
vite the question whether hybrid form, rather than marking a departure from
popular, mainstream cinema, as is often thought to be the case in the United
States, actually constitutes the heart or essence of such cinema. Contending
that Hong Kong cinema since the 1970s "has been arguably the world's most
energetic, imaginative popular cinema,"[5] David Bordwell characterizes popular cinema generally as possessing features I have associated in this book with
hybrid form. He refers, for instance, to popular cinema's "scavenger aesthetic": individual films in quest of "striking moments" commonly extract
and adapt images and motifs from other works, even if such elements do not
always cohere in the new context.[6] He also regards popular cinema as a
medium of "mixed emotions" (and cites its "reckless mix of moods"), rather
than simply of "pure states of feeling."[7] Popular cinema in his view "delights"
in "very diverse splendors," in "kaleidoscopic variety in terms of events as well
as emotions."[8]

Such emphasis on popular cinema's complexity complements a 1996 *Art
Forum* essay by Howard Hampton that highlights the prominence of *stylistic*
diversity as well as diversity of events and emotions—at least in Hong Kong's
popular cinema. Praising *Chungking Express* (1994), Wong Kar-wai's critically
acclaimed, if not commercially successful, Hong Kong film produced by
Quentin Tarantino, as a "dazzlingly adroit synthesis of art cinema and MTV,"
the essay casts Wong Kar-wai's esthetic as "a logical outgrowth of the Hong
Kong reanimator mode: fusing wildly disparate styles and taking them to sublime extremes."[9] Such underscoring of disparate styles agrees with my conception of hybrid form, which focuses on admixtures of diverse styles and
genres as well as of disparate events and emotions. Further, as indicated in my
introduction, hybrid cinema's shifting emotions, events, genres, and styles

tend to spur tension and disorientation in the spectator, especially when these shifts seem illogical, unexplained, or—to use Hampton's word—wild.

By "hybrid form" I have also meant the practice, which subsumes the "scavenger aesthetic," of films citing and quoting other films of varying levels of quality. That Wong Kar-wai's work, as an example, fills the bill is suggested by a question, similar to ones raised about Tarantino's cinema, that scholar Peter Brunette put to the director: ". . . is it fair to say that your films are ultimately about other films, rather than about real life?" Wong replied, "They're about real life."[10] Brunette's query, of course, brings up other questions relevant to hybrid form: Can an artwork ever *not* be about real life? Is it likely that historical changes in how people regard themselves and the world will *not* inflect artistic form? Motion pictures in my view inevitably bear on real life, even when they busily cite other films and genres, take dream-like and nonsensical paths in the manner of *Un Chien andalou* and *Entr'acte*, or pursue abstract, non-figurative directions as do films by artists like Oskar Fischinger, Harry Smith, and Jordan Belson. Similarly, music, dance, and abstract painting and sculpture inevitably relate to political, psychological, and other dimensions of the reality from which they emerge. Especially given the blurring of lines between art, life, politics, and entertainment in today's media-drenched world, hybrid cinema's invocations of diverse films and other works of art and entertainment relate almost inevitably—as, we shall see, Pedro Almodóvar insists—to the real-life experiences of both creative artists and the general public.

Shaolin Soccer

Shaolin Soccer bulges with diverse stylistic and generic references. One review found the film "crammed with pastiche, paying tribute to Sergio Leone westerns, 1970s bad-hair musicals, and Bruce Lee. . . ."[11] *Shaolin* also alludes to war films, gross-out comedies, various musicals, sports films, films about criminality in sports, science fiction, and a range of films deploying flashy, computer-generated special effects.

When Sing (Stephen Chow), leader of a soccer team comprised of erstwhile kung fu students, finds himself pummeled by sadistic rivals in a training match, he suddenly appears wearing a soldier's helmet, brandishing an automatic rifle, and scrambling under barbed wire. As bullets streak by and explosives pound overhead, he shouts into a huge mobile phone to seek reinforcements. Then a straight cut to a new shot reveals him holding just a sneaker rather than the phone, and a stick instead of the rifle. The fantasy is ratified by Sing's crippled soccer coach Fung (Ng Man Tat) gravely proclaiming, "This game is war."

Earlier, marveling on a street corner at the kung fu skills of a steam-buns maker as she kneads dough and twirls it into the sky, Sing breaks into song— "I sing to express my admiration"—and bystanders suddenly materialize beside him and vault into dance. The homely buns maker, Mui (Vicki Zhao), soon falls in love with Sing, but he hesitates to reciprocate. Nevertheless, near film's end Mui saves Sing's team from disaster in the championship match against "Team Evil," whose members have been rendered nearly invincible by illegal drugs furnished by Hung (Patrick Tse Yin), their corrupt coach. Turning up on the soccer field transformed into a pristine blend of E.T. and Joan of Arc, Mui declares herself ready to serve on Sing's team, which, since it has lost players to injury or death in this brutal match, desperately needs a replacement so as to maintain the number necessary to stay in the game. In addition to her body, Mui brings fresh, tai chi-like tactics to the match; preternaturally calm, ethereal, and steely, she leads Sing and his teammates to victory against all odds. Then to conclude the film she and Sing appear together as the "Kung Fu Couple" on the cover of *Time* magazine and on a poster presiding over downtown Hong Kong. No more sublime than this romantic duo were Gene Kelly and Debbie Reynolds in the billboard image culminating *Singin' in the Rain* (1952, Gene Kelly and Stanley Donen).

Sing's soccer wars are enlivened with computer-generated morphing—for example, a soaring soccer ball turns into fire and then into a fiery lion. Such magical changes signify the power and glory of kung fu more than of soccer or, once Mui enters the story, of romance. The first significant blurring, wrinkling, and morphing into fire of a solid object occurs early in *Shaolin Soccer* when Sing explains that his devotion to kung fu began as he watched Bruce Lee on television long ago. (He also devotes his only direct address to the camera—and to the audience of *Shaolin Soccer*—to extolling kung fu.) Sing regards kung fu as key not merely to all martial arts, but to the ideal fusion of the human mind and body, and consequently to universal perfection. Soccer for him, like song, dance, and, implicitly, computer magic, exists to celebrate and advertise—or as he says, "package"—kung fu.

Opposing Sing are not only corrupt soccer players and coaches who employ dirty tricks to win, but, more generally, individuals who cling to meager conceptions of reality. "You people are demented. Get back to reality," shrieks the killjoy owner of the sweet-bun stand where Mui works, when Chow, soon joined by bystanders, breaks into song and dance inspired by Mui's kung fu skills. Later, as Sing tries to persuade Iron Head, one of his former kung fu brothers who has fallen into poverty and lost all self-respect, to take up kung fu again, the downtrodden older man replies, "I've already advised you to live in a down-to-earth manner. . . . There's a vacancy cleaning toilets. It should be good for you to take it rather than to dream anything." Sing replies that it is distinctly human to dream.

In the name of kung fu, then, not only Sing, Mui, soccer, and romance triumph at the end of this hybrid action comedy, but also music, dance, dream, imagination, and humanness itself. The film's streak of self-parody tends not to reverse the triumphal tide, but to lend it intelligence and self-awareness. If anything counters the "feel-good" momentum, aside from the impoverished view of reality held by Mui's mean boss and Iron Head, it is the degradation suffered by Iron Head, Mui, and Fung. Iron Head's demoralization persists even after he joins Sing's kung fu soccer squad. At the nadir of the same training match that propels Sing into the war fantasy, Iron Head moans, "I am old and ugly and with no dignity." Only after this grim admission does he, along with his teammates, experience the miraculous infusion of kung fu pride and energy that sets them on course to victory.

Instances of degradation and self-renunciation in *Shaolin Soccer* begin early. The first scene in the Hong Kong version of the film reveals Hung and Fung in their youth, about twenty years prior to the main action, heatedly conversing in a dark locker room photographed in black-and-white (unlike the remainder of the film, which is in color). A star soccer player at that time, Fung berates Hung, a petty criminal, for insulting him by offering him a bribe. But as Hung cowers before him, Fung concludes his tirade by snatching a check from Hung's hand. Unlike Butch in *Pulp Fiction*, Fung takes the bribe after all; whereupon Hung kneels, allowing Fung, known to soccer fans as Golden Leg, to set his foot on Hung's head, the more easily to fasten his shoelaces. Then on the soccer field in the next shot, still in black-and-white, Fung deliberately misses the kick; among the patrons and fans who charge angrily toward him, thugs paid by Hung break Fung's leg. Hung smirks and strides away; and, through a dissolve, continues smirking and striding, in color in the present day, now an older, more successful sports entrepreneur. Reporters besiege him in the present for explanations of his success as coach and owner of Team Evil, soccer champions for five years. Then Fung hobbles into frame to beg Hung for a chance to coach, having worked for him faithfully for two decades. In a reversal of positions they occupied at the end of the opening scene, the crippled, groveling Fung lowers his head to the ground so that Hung can prop his foot on it. Hung rejects Fung's request to coach, though, and brutally informs him that the men who fractured his leg twenty years earlier did so on Hung's orders.

In subsequent scenes, after he has evidently left Hung's employ, Fung remains an enigmatic figure: at times he seems lost and defeated, even after he starts to coach Sing's kung fu soccer team, while at other moments he appears more playful and buoyant, as when he describes himself as a philosopher and a member of the intellectual class in his initial encounter with Sing. Further, in Sing's fantasy of pre-modern kung fu glory in the middle of this encounter, Fung is cast as a charismatic wizard performing kung fu in front of a temple. Then Sing himself appears within the fantasy, directly addressing the audience as well as Fung on the virtues of kung fu; next, Fung magisterially pops up in his wizard costume on the commercial street where his encounter with Sing is occurring. Thus Fung exhibits in a short span of film notable emotive and sartorial range. Like the image of his brazen, youthful hypocrisy at the start of the film, however, his degradation, along with that of Iron Head and Mui, is never quite erased by the feel-good tide that sweeps through *Shaolin Soccer*. Instead, the pain endured by Fung, Iron Head, and Mui contributes to tensions or dualities of triumph and defeat, fulfillment and self-abnegation, which color the entirety of this action comedy's hybrid course.

The World, Tokyo Story, and *Umberto D*

Human failure and degradation become pervasive in *The World*, a film that develops one strand of hybrid form in particular: citing, quoting, and imitating notable works of art and culture. The film observes the decline of hope and energy among young, unwed Chinese men and women who have come from distant, rural areas to work for meager wages in a bustling theme park in suburban Beijing. Boasting that visitors can "see the world without leaving Beijing," the park features scaled-down replicas of world-famous sites such as the Eiffel Tower, the Taj Majal, London Bridge, the Pyramids, and the Lower Manhattan skyline. The fact that a visitor can circle all these replicas in just 15 minutes on the park's two-car monorail, and that the replicas stand within view of each other, can be taken to suggest the shrinking of today's world, in which air-planes, cell phones, and the Internet bring disparate peoples, places, and events ever closer together. But to the young employees, including dancers, security guards, and elevator operators—each of whom possesses a cell phone, by the way—the park represents estrangement from the world. This place of employ-ment that cites or quotes other places somewhat as hybrid cinema cites or quotes other films provides scant uplift or inspiration to its employees. Rather, their repeated sightings of replicas remind them that, having been unable to make a life for themselves where they were born and grew up in China, and now feeling out of place in Beijing, they lack resources such as money and pass-ports that would enable them to visit the original sites—and the peoples and cultures associated with them—on which the replicas are based. Thus, while young female dancers in sparkling costumes evoke India and other fabled do-mains before large groups of tourists, the performers do not anticipate travel-ing far beyond the park, which includes crowded hovels in which they dwell near the spiffy replicas as well as an immense auditorium for glitzy stage shows. The falsity, enclosure, and immobility within the park deplete and alienate the male and female employees emotionally and physically. Perhaps this is why, when Tao (Tao Zhao) tells her lover and fellow worker, Taisheng (Chen Taishen), that she would not want to live without him, he replies listlessly, "You can't count on anyone these days. Don't think so much of me."

While focusing on a theme park that exists to evoke other places, *The World* alludes to other films and types of film, including cartoons, backstage musi-cals, and the cinema of Yasujiro Ozu, especially *Tokyo Story* (1953). Ozu's in-ternationally popular film depicts an elderly Japanese couple who, on a trip to Tokyo to visit their married children, come to feel they have no place either in their children's lives or in the broader world. In Jia Zhang-ke's film, an elderly Chinese couple travels to Beijing, where their son has died in an industrial ac-cident, and they sit bereft and silent as they are handed cash in compensation for his death from the company that employed him. An unhappy tune from Ozu's cinema rises as the father impassively accepts the envelope containing the money.

At times the inertness of this grieving couple is matched by that of youth-ful characters in *The World*. When Tao and Taisheng talk fully-clothed in bed early in the film, their physical movements and their dialogue are minimal and enervated. Adding to the impression of inertness is the stationary camera, which views the action in both long shot and long take—no editing either disrupts or energizes the scene's space and time. Similar combinations of long shots and long takes (along with low-angle camera positions) are frequent in Ozu's cinema; and as often occurs in Ozu, the camera's still, distant, unedited view of Tao and Taisheng in *The World* tends to underscore the characters' inhibited circumstances. Indeed, the sustained long shot of Tao and Taisheng makes it difficult to detect facial expressions that might contradict the sense that these individuals are depleted, emotionally frozen, and remote from one another despite their physical proximity. Rather than seeming merely intractable, however, the static long take/long shot of the two young people in love who find themselves immersed in blank, dreary sensations feels painfully patient and delicate. Such complexity helps account for film critic Manohla Dargis's statement that Jia Zhang-ke is "one of the world's most important filmmakers whose work most likely will never make it to a theater near you."[12]

Later the relationship of Tao and Taisheng picks up a bit when, attired respectively in the uniforms of a flight attendant and a pilot, they neck in the pilot's seat of a mock airplane at the park. Yet again their interaction remains muted, ostensibly because someone might see or interrupt them in this public space. Again, the rule of falsity, enclosure, and immobility prevails. The cockpit is a replica; the characters are not truly airline employees; the plane does not fly. Passion is stanched; the main action is inaction. At other moments, Tao remarks that she has never known anyone who has flown, and she is unaware that a plane passing overhead carries her Russian friend Anna. But like other characters in *The World*, Tao longs to fly, a desire realized in a cartoon of her soaring through space in the airline uniform after her cell phone rings with a text message. She also appears to fly with Taisheng in the magic carpet ride, a park amusement utilizing rear-screen images to create the illusion of human subjects floating up to the top of the Eiffel Tower. Not only are the customers in this scenario in fact stationary, but Tao and Taisheng, rarely if ever content, are persuaded to feign happiness by the technician who films them with a digital camera against the phony moving backdrop. An adjacent monitor displays the resulting image that is false both to physical and emotional reality. It remains the cell-phone-triggered cartoons that depict most delightfully and convincingly uninhibited mobility and other pleasures denied the characters in real life.

Convergences between *The World*'s cartoon fantasies and its predominant realism are central to its hybrid form. Unlike backstage musicals such as *42nd Street* and *Gold Diggers of 1933*, *The World* does not forsake natural laws of space and time in its stage shows, which, though glamorous, are gravity-bound. The cartoons take up the slack by creating fantastic universes akin to those of Busby Berkeley; simultaneously, the cartoons serve to underscore the film's essential realism, which brings to mind Italian Neorealism as well as Ozu's cinema.

As I have noted, realism in *The World* favors long takes, long shots, and a stationary camera, all of which tend to allow the action on screen to evolve as in everyday life—naturally and continuously, with minimal manipulation of space and time, and minimal reference to filmmaking tools, such as cameras and editing devices. Further, in focusing on inaction or decidedly mundane conduct, *The World* harks back to descriptions of Italian Neorealism by André Bazin and Cesare Zavattini. A primary instance for Bazin of minimal and mundane activity is the maid Maria waking up one morning in *Umberto D* (1951, Vittorio De Sica). "The narrative unit . . . is the succession of concrete instants of life," he writes. "The camera confines itself to watching her doing her little chores: moving around the kitchen. . . ." Bazin then praises the film-maker's refusal to skip, possibly in the interest of narrative or dramatic intensity, any of these chores or concrete instants: "The cinema here is conceived as the exact opposite of that 'art of ellipsis' to which we are much too ready to believe it devoted. Ellipsis is a narrative process; it is logical in nature and so it is abstract as well; it presupposes analysis and choice; it organizes the facts in accord with the general dramatic direction to which it forces them to submit. . . ." Instead, argues Bazin, De Sica in this scene accents what other directors might consider dramatically trivial—he "divides" the ordinary event of waking up, "moving around the kitchen," and making coffee, "into smaller events and these into events smaller still, to the extreme limits of our capacity to perceive them in time. . . . Have I already said that it is Zavattini's dream [Zavattini co-authored the screenplay] to make a whole film out of ninety minutes in the life of a man to whom nothing happens?"[13]

Yet much does happen in *Umberto D*. Just moments prior to the scene in which she wakes up, for example, impoverished Maria quietly realizes that she is pregnant, that holding the father accountable will be impossible, and that as a single mother she will likely be evicted from her apartment. Not particularly fortunate either is old Umberto, who befriends Maria yet keeps his distance; he too faces eviction, since he cannot pay his rent on his paltry pension. As the film begins, he joins a futile march in Rome protesting inadequate pensions; and by film's end, he attempts suicide on a railroad track. De Sica saw this work, his favorite among his films, as addressing "the tragedy of those people who find themselves cut off from a world that they nevertheless helped to build, a tragedy hidden by resignation and silence but one that occasionally explodes in loud demonstrations or that is pushed into appalling suicides."[14]

We might similarly regard *The World* as a film about "people who find themselves cut off," and as depicting a "tragedy hidden by resignation and silence"—hence what I have termed the enervation and inaction of the main characters, observed by Jia Zhang-ke with a candor more than equal to De Sica's. Further, as in *Umberto D*, though action is minimal and events proceed slowly in *The World*, things do happen. Not only does a young man die in an industrial accident off-screen, for instance, but Tao and Taisheng die off-screen as well. As their shrouded bodies observed in long shot are carried on stretchers down a dark outdoor stairwell and set down on the cold ground, bystanders suggest they have perished from a gas leak in the apartment where they slept.

But it is not certain their deaths are entirely accidental. At the wedding of her friend Wei (Jue Jing), Tao has learned that Taisheng has been seeing another woman. The film's spectator knows that while his exchanges with this woman, a dressmaker named Qun (Yi-qun Wang), have been playful, they have not been much more passionate than his meetings with Tao. Further, Qun is married, and longs to see her husband who fled illegally to France years earlier. Knowing Qun only as a text message on Taisheng's cell phone, however, Tao grows fearful and despondent. She tries on a transparent raincoat that prefigures her encasement in death; then she lies restlessly in bed, not unlike Maria in *Umberto D*. Finally, Tao goes to Wei's vacant apartment to spend the night, and there Taisheng finds her. The most tumultuous outbursts involving romance in *The World* have occurred between Wei and her jealous boyfriend Niu (Zhong-wei Jiang); enraged at one point after Wei has failed to answer his cell-phone calls, Niu has even set himself on fire. Yet it is these two individuals who become husband and wife in *The World*. Tao never receives passion such as Niu expresses for Wei; and Tao is denied as well the surprisingly sweet outcome of the often tawdry feuding between Wei and Niu. Possibly convinced that nothing could be less fulfilling than what she has called life, Tao longs for death, which in her desperation may represent, a bit like *The World*'s marvelous cartoons, release from hardship and paralysis and even a renewal of energy. Voice-over at *The World*'s end, in any case, Tao and Taisheng exchange final words while the camera angles slightly closer to their dead bodies on the ground: "Are we dead?" asks Taisheng. "No," she replies, "this is just the beginning."

Run Lola Run

Run Lola Run, a film markedly different from *The World*, begins by quoting a statement that in its challenge to routine notions of beginnings and endings brings to mind the final exchange between Tao and Taisheng: "After the game is before the game," reads the decree in *Lola*, which is credited to Sepp Herberger, the talented coach who guided Germany in 1954 to its first world soccer championship against a reputedly invincible Hungarian team. Herberger's assertion that seemingly distinct and contrary conditions coincide when it comes to the game of soccer may apply as well to hybrid cinema. A review of *Run Lola Run*, when this film opened the 1999 New Directors/New Films series in New York City, referred to its "tirelessly shifting styles";[15] and indeed Tykwer's film contains more overlaps of diverse moods, styles, and genres than many another hybrid film, including *The World*. The German film tells the story of young Lola's (Franka Potente) race to raise 100,000 marks, and deliver it to her boyfriend Manni (Moritz Bleibtreu) by noon—in just 20 minutes, so that his gangster boss will not kill him. In a desperate phone call to Lola buttressed by flashbacks in black-and-white, Manni has explained that he received the 100,000 in payment for drugs, but left the money in a bag on a train, where a homeless man picked it up. Lola's effort to rescue Manni, intercut with his own attempt to find 100,000 marks, is portrayed three times—each with distinctly different details and conclusions, though each portrayal juxtaposes animation and live action, and each invokes multiple genres, including music video, art cinema, science fiction, crime thriller, teen romance, soap opera, melodrama, comedy, and farce.

At the end of the introduction to *Run Lola Run* that begins with Herberger's enigmatic assertion, a figure who turns out to be a security guard at the bank where Lola's father is an executive kicks a soccer ball into the sky, prompting an aerial view of a mostly nondescript crowd of people who have

Run Lola Run *combines aspects of art cinema with allusions to traditional last-minute rescues and interactive cyber-narratives. Sony Pictures Classics/The Kobal Collection/Spauke, Bernd.*

been moving about aimlessly, often in fast motion, while a male voice-over has puzzled over the enigma of human existence: "Man is probably the most mysterious species on our planet—a mystery of unanswered questions. Who are we? Where do we come from? Where are we going? How do we know what we think we know? Why do we believe anything at all?" These voice-over questions have succeeded the printed quotation not only of Herberger's statement but also of one by T. S. Eliot (which was cited by former U.S. Secretary of Defense Robert S. McNamara in *The Fog of War*): "We shall not cease from exploration and the end of all our exploring will be to arrive where we started and know the place for the first time." This statement from Eliot's *Burnt Norton* perhaps supports the hope that human bewilderment eventually yields to knowledge. In contrast, the voice-over commentator in *Run Lola Run* sees only "countless questions in search of an answer . . . an answer . . . will give rise to a new question . . . the next answer will give rise to the next question and so on." Finally, however, the voice suggests a way out of the conundrum: "But, in the end, isn't it always the same question? And always the same answer? The ball is round. The game lasts 90 minutes. That's a fact." It is at this moment that the security guard appears on screen, declares that "Everything else is theory," and kicks the ball toward the camera in the sky. In the subsequent aerial shot, the shapeless crowd of people, just multi-colored dots when viewed from above, congeals into the film's title, suggesting that life may acquire form or definition through this film, though just for as long as the film lasts and according to rules and boundaries of its particular system or game. The film will displace, in a sense, the vast enigma of existence with one more finite and graspable; and rather than grieve over humankind's lot, *Run Lola Run*, like hybrid films by Tarantino and other directors, will take a light, gamy tack.

"The ball is round," an assertion of fact and form that, like the initial printed statement, has been ascribed to Herberger,[16] adds to the introduction's soccer references, which are linked at key narrative moments to various objects such as telephones and bags of money that soar up and down like soccer balls. Although soccer is far less central to *Run Lola Run* than to *Shaolin Soccer*, references to soccer in the German film inaugurate highly athletic human and cinematic activity, such as Lola's almost ceaseless running, rapid editing, jump cuts, split screens, swooping zooms, camera moves, changes of color, and computer-generated effects. In other ways as well, soccer seems comparable to the cinema in *Run Lola Run*. The sport obviously enjoys a world-wide audience, much as movies do. The security guard who declares the ball to be round and launches it skyward seems almost a magnet around which the restless, motley crowd gathers or finds a center. *Run Lola Run*, in turn, pulls together diverse artistic styles and dispositions likely to attract, as soccer does, a range of popular as well as highbrow sensibilities.

Soccer's importance at the outset of *Run Lola Run* brings to mind another celebrated German film, *The Marriage of Maria Braun* (1979, Rainer Werner Fassbinder), in which soccer plays a key role. Braun's house explodes at the end of the film as she turns up her kitchen burner to light a cigarette after she has left the gas on—and as her radio blares the crowd's ecstatic reaction to Germany's defeat of Hungary in the 1954 soccer championship. Like Lola, Tao, and Maria in *Umberto D*, Braun has been seeking happiness in a country growing increasingly prosperous, powerful, media-minded, capitalistic, and proud—and these developments are encapsulated in the soccer victory. But like Lola and Tao, Maria Braun dies following an ordeal or grave disappointment related to the man she loves. As with Tao and Taisheng, moreover, whether Braun and her husband die accidentally or deliberately when the house blows up remains unclear—one of "countless questions in search of an answer."

In *Run Lola Run*, Lola dies in the first depiction of her adventure while trying to help Manni, yet she also lives on, and then opts for a second round, which, it turns out, diverges from the first. Instantly upon her death at the end of the first account, we not only hear her voice, as with Tao, but also see her alive, sensual, lolling in bed with Manni, seeking assurance of his love. Next she declares her refusal to die, thus initiating the second version of the saga, in which Manni is the one to die, though again the two converse in bed in an orange haze, with Manni being the one to seek assurance of love. Lola then pronounces him undead, whereupon a third round of the basic plot begins. The reversal of death in this film, or the representation of life in death, is perhaps less poignant than in *The World*, partly because the turnaround or convergence in *Run Lola Run* seems but one more arbitrary move in its play with cinematic form as well as with reality. The borders between life and death in this game staged for spectators around the globe remain significant, but perhaps they are no more sacred than those between film genres.

Among the many genres evoked in *Run Lola Run*, family melodrama undergoes some of the funniest twists, which primarily involve Lola's father (Herbert Knaup), though her mother (Ute Lubosch) appears first in the film. Each time Lola races out of her apartment to help Manni, she passes her daft mother, who asks her to bring back shampoo, then tells someone on the phone, "But you're married too." Meanwhile, the TV in front of Lola's mother displays Lola as a cartoon figure, running down a stairway past a toothy man and his dog after she leaves the apartment.

In the first two portrayals of Lola's quest, she eventually lands in the office of her banker-father to ask for money. Prior to her arrival the first time, her running through city streets is broken by static, grainy, hand-held shots of her father in his office mired in tense, soap-opera-like dialogue with his mistress (Nina Petri), who indicates she is pregnant, and apparently wants him to leave his wife. She says that "it's worst at night" when she wakes up alone, unable to sleep. When Lola, after more running, barges into the office and discovers the illicit couple, she not only asks for money, but screams in exasperation, shattering the glass above a clock. Undaunted, the father marches Lola out of the office and tells her to inform her mother he is leaving the family, which he says has failed to appreciate him. Further, he huffily asserts he is not Lola's father. How could he be, he adds, given that she is a "weirdo" and a "cuckoo's egg"?

While the father is dominant in this scene, power shifts to his mistress and to Lola in the second version of the saga. Now the father looks shaken and deflated when the mistress, after telling him she is pregnant, and asking whether he wants to have a baby with her, divulges that the child is not his. Soon Lola enters, calls the mistress a cow, and gets slapped by her father. But Lola fights back, and gains the upper hand, initially by hurling objects at her father, and then by returning with a gun snatched from the holster of the bank's security guard (the same who kicked the ball in the introduction). Lola next marches her father out of the office at gunpoint, having fired two warning shots over his head, and down to the bank vault, where she destroys the entry keypad with more gunfire.

In the third version of the story, family melodrama recedes, as the exchange between Lola's father and his mistress is abbreviated, and no meeting at all occurs between Lola and her father. The latter reacts happily to his mistress's news of the pregnancy, apparently assuming the child to be his, and then leaves quickly for an appointment with his business friend, Mr. Meier (Ludger Pistor). The father drives off with Meier just as Lola appears on the street and vainly calls after him. Meier tells Lola's father that he has decided against having children because he works hard and would have little time to see them. His statement echoes the father's remark in the first version of the story that his family complains that he works too hard. To some degree, thoughts percolate and grow contagious in this film. Another instance occurs when in the frantic opening phone conversation between Manni and Lola, both teenagers suddenly think of the bag of money Manni left on the train seat, and then repeatedly say, "the bag"—whereupon the film cuts back to the bum who noticed Manni leaving the train, and who with a look of revelation now says, "the bag," and heads toward it.

More significant than any contagion of thought in *Run Lola Run*, however, is the power of desire, conjecture, and imagination to transform the world— or, as in *Last Year at Marienbad* (1961, Alain Resnais), to generate images that may be false to external reality. The force of Lola's desire turns death into life, and undoes the past. Further, in the gambling casino in the third version of Lola's adventure, the screams of her desire shatter wine glasses held by the elegant patrons, freeze these patrons in their tracks, and cause the little roulette ball (yet another round ball) to settle on Lola's number every time the spinning disc comes to rest, thereby allowing her to win 100,000 marks. When Manni breathlessly tells Lola on the phone that the bum has probably gone far off with the money—"to Canada or Hong Kong or Bermuda or whatever"— post-card-like aerial views representing these places flash by. And when Manni warns Lola that his boss will punish him because he will think Manni is withholding the money, images of what Manni fears appear on screen. When, after Manni's phone call to her in the first version of the tale, Lola rapidly ponders whom to ask for help, numerous characters appear in cameo fashion, including her father shaking his head "no."

Finally, when Lola passes three minor characters, who have few if any lines to speak, as she races through the city and the bank, the term "and then" appears on screen, followed by still photographs of each character's subsequent life. But the photographs vary with each version of the story. A minor character turns to religion and helping the poor in one version, for instance, but wins a lottery and becomes flamboyantly narcissistic in another. Perhaps such extended treatment of minor characters reflects Lola's fleeting conjectures as she rushes by. Or, such images possibly address the curiosity of the film's spectator, who must wonder, however subliminally, "Who are these minor characters, or extras—individuals who perhaps resemble me more than the film's stars do? And what becomes of them?" In addition, lending narrative attention to characters ordinarily denied it may be one more way *Run Lola Run* departs from convention, while also raising questions about the quality of attention that strangers, friends, and foes accord each other in daily life, as on the silver screen.

Talk to Her

As in *Run Lola Run*, desire and fantasy run up against reality and reason in Pedro Almodóvar's films, including the critically acclaimed *Talk to Her* (2002), winner of the Academy Award for Best Original Screenplay and the Golden Globe Award for Best Foreign Language Film. Following *Talk to Her*'s U.S. opening, *New York Times* critic A. O. Scott declared it "by far the most complex, layered narrative Mr. Almodóvar has attempted," a film of "daunting dramatic scope and breathtaking coherence."[17] Before focusing on the scope of hybrid form in *Talk to Her*, I would like to consider the commitments to such form evident in Almodóvar's work generally, as he and his admirers have been quick to point out.

"My hope is to meld reality and fantasy," Almodóvar told an interviewer in 2004,[18] adding, "I was . . . very influenced by Buñuel and Surrealism. . . . We both have a sense of the irrational, the extraordinary taking place in daily life. That particular point of view is specific to Spain."[19] Linking his cinematic sensibility to the Spanish temperament earlier in his career, in 1987, Almodóvar observed: "Intuition and imagination influence us more than reason. . . . We don't fear disorder and chaos."[20] As for affinities to U.S. hybrid films in which fantasy and disorder are prominent, Almodóvar stressed in 2004 his high regard for Tarantino's *Kill Bill*;[21] and in 1987 he said, ". . . I recognize myself a lot in *Blue Velvet*. I love it."[22] In a recent analysis of Buñuel's *Belle de Jour*, literary and cultural critic Michael Wood states that "Buñuel wants to insist on the permeability of the worlds of reality and dream, and on their equal status as objects of interest and aspects of lived life."[23] Similarly, Almodóvar's cinema underscores the permeability of reality and fantasy as well as the distortions of reality wrought by excesses of desire and imagination.

Besides stressing his intention to meld reality and fantasy, Almodóvar has pointed to the mergence in his work of multiple genres, including comedy, farce, tragedy, soap opera, melodrama, horror, film noir, romance, science fiction, and even—in *Live Flesh* (1997), for example—political cinema. In *Talk to Her*, Almodóvar also incorporates silent cinema via the *Shrinking Lover*, a short film of comic horror that he wrote and directed, and that is followed by a splash of abstract animation. As important to him as the diversity of generic allusions in his cinema, however, is the speed and ease with which these allusions verge into one another. "You can say my films are melodramas, tragicomedies, comedies or whatever," he tells one interlocutor, "because I . . . put everything together and even change genre within the same sequence and very quickly."[24] He stipulates in another interview: "When mixing genres, the shift in tone . . . has to flow. . . ."[25]

Almodóvar's interviewers tend to agree with him. Marsha Kinder, for example, notes that agile generic shifts and convergences in his cinema strongly contribute to its distinctiveness: "It seems to me that what lies at the center of your unique tone is . . . that fluidity with which you move so quickly from one genre to another, or from one feeling or tone to another. . . ."[26] While Kinder's statement appears in an interview she conducted with Almodóvar in 1987, her focus on the fluidity and quickness of his shifts of genre and tone is echoed years later by other commentators. Guillermo Altares points to the speed of

Almodóvar's moves in *All about My Mother* (1999), winner of Hollywood's Oscar for Best Foreign Film, when he describes it as "a tragedy that all of a sudden turns into a comedy."[27] Lynn Hirschberg stresses fluidity in 2004, when she describes Almodóvar's address of gender and sexuality, perhaps with films such as *The Law of Desire* (1987) and *All about My Mother* in mind: ". . . he depicts gender and sexuality as fluid: in Almodóvar's world, women were once men; men pose as women; transsexuals can be fathers or mothers"—his characters are ever "shifting."[28] In summary, Almodóvar and these commentators suggest not only that agile shifts and convergences are central to his cinema, but that this pattern extends beyond genre to sexuality, gender, and other key aspects of human identity—as well as to the interplay of reality and fantasy.

Offering yet another signpost for exploring his work, Almodóvar states that ". . . the moral of all my films is to get to a stage of greater freedom."[29] This freedom does not come about, he states, solely because he transgresses or dissolves borders between film genres, facets of human identity, and realms of human experience. Rather, as when he says that shifts in tone must flow, or speaks of "gut feeling"[30] and "naturalness,"[31] or asserts that "the fiercest humor and the most terrible events come together in life; and that's what life is all about,"[32] he underscores that shifts and convergences in his cinema succeed because they are anything but artificial and arbitrary. They succeed because they are faithful to the pulse and truth of the filmmaker, his characters, and their worlds.

Almodóvar's focus on freedom as truth to oneself, and as the unobstructed expression or objectification of this truth in art, is evident also when he discusses his purpose in citing and quoting in his films artistic works by authors, directors, and choreographers he respects—for instance, *The Criminal Life of Archibaldo de la Cruz* (1955, Luis Buñuel) in *Live Flesh*; *All about Eve* (1950, Joseph L. Mankiewicz) and *A Streetcar Named Desire* (Tennessee Williams, 1947) in *All about My Mother*; dance pieces by German choreographer Pina Bausch at the start and end of *Talk to Her*. Almodóvar invokes such works not chiefly to "pay tribute,"[33] he insists, but to get at a feeling or condition that has become part of his own experience. "I never cite a film as . . . homage or . . . quotation. I cite cinema as if the films I have seen were part of my life and of my experience."[34] In addition to underscoring freedom, truth, and fidelity to life and experience, Almodóvar speaks of "private morality"[35] and of "the moral of all my films." Many directors juggle diverse genres and quotations, he suggests, but each one does so differently, guided by his or her private morality or personality—which is probably a fair way of defining an auteur. Almodóvar must—and can only—be himself.

Central to the convergence of reality and fantasy in *Talk to Her*, to the fluid shifts of genre and identity, and to the operation of Almodóvar's private morality, is the nurse Benigno Martín (Javier Cámara), whose imaginative reconstruction of the world leads to his imprisonment and suicide, but also, perhaps, to the awakening of a beautiful young woman, the dancer Alicia (Leonor Watling), who has been in a deep coma for four years following a traffic accident. In a climactic conversation toward film's end, Benigno informs his friend Marco (Darío Grandinetti) of his resolve to marry the still unconscious Alicia, whom he has cared for in the hospital since her accident. When Marco, a journalist, says that Benigno's proposal is crazy, Benigno counters that it makes good sense: he and Alicia "get along better than most married couples. Why shouldn't a man want to marry the woman he loves?" Marco replies: "Because the woman is in a coma. Because Alicia can't say with any part of her body: 'I do.' Because we don't know if vegetative life is really life. Your relationship with Alicia is a monologue and it's insane."

Later, when Marco visits him in prison and the two talk again, Benigno tells him how much he has enjoyed reading a travel guide Marco wrote about Havana. "I really identified with those people who've got nothing and invent everything" says the prisoner, adding a moment later: "When you describe that Cuban woman leaning out a window . . . waiting uselessly, seeing how time passes and nothing happens . . . I thought that woman was me." Possibly Benigno refers just to his existence in prison without Alicia, but his comment also bears on his earlier life.

Indeed, his inclination to invent everything because he has nothing, to invent a dialogue with Alicia out of a monologue, to speak for her in her silence, to allow his desires and fantasies to outrun reality, begins well before chance brings the stricken Alicia to the hospital where he works. He falls in love with her not only prior to her accident, but before he has any exchange with her at all, as he watches her obsessively through his apartment window taking dance lessons in the glass-walled academy across the street. He has lived in his apartment for twenty years with his elderly mother, ministering to her somewhat as he will later care for Alicia—cutting her hair, for example, and scrubbing "her down well, front and back," as he tells a psychiatrist. The mother never appears in the film, though; she simply is heard, reproving Benigno for hovering too long at the window watching Alicia dance. It is after his mother dies that Benigno visits the psychiatrist, who happens to be Alicia's father, and who maintains an office in the flat where Alicia lives. Following the psychiatric interview, the enchanted Benigno steals into Alicia's room, then assures her he is "harmless" when she emerges startled from the shower. Earlier, he catches up to her on the street below his apartment to hand her a wallet she has dropped, and she tells him as they walk—he has asked to accompany her, noting he has nothing to do—of her passion for travel and film, especially silent film. He informs her he does not go out much, as he has been caring for his mother until her recent death. In these exchanges between Alicia and Benigno on the street and in her apartment, the vibrant dancer exhibits no interest in romance, or even friendship, with him. In the apartment, she primarily seems taken aback. If he requires a more positive response from her, he must invent one.

Eventually Benigno invents a "relationship," as Marco puts it, so loving that he impregnates his unconscious patient, whereupon society deems him a monster and a criminal. Yet what stand out before his fantasies lead to criminality are his goodness and generosity. As the curtain rises in a theatre at the start of *Talk to Her*, Benigno observes Nina Bausch and another female dancer stagger in mute anguish with their eyes closed across the stage, while a stranger (Marco) in the seat next to him weeps. As Benigno in the subsequent scene trims Alicia's nails and massages her hands in her hospital room, he recounts the sad beauty of his theatre experience—the haggard dancers, their male assistant frantically pushing tables and chairs out of their way, the man next to Benigno "crying from emotion." Enlivened by both this memory and Alicia's presence, Benigno proceeds to show his patient, whose eyes remain closed like the dancers' eyes, and whose attire is white like theirs, his splendid surprise, a photograph of Bausch that this famous dancer and choreographer has inscribed to Alicia, almost certainly at Benigno's request: "I hope you overcome all your obstacles and start dancing." Yet more evidence of Benigno's compassion and thoughtfulness arises when he offers to work extra shifts at night caring for Alicia so that his female colleague Matilde (Lola Dueñas), whose husband has just left her, can stay home with her children.

In *Kill Bill Vol. 1*, The Bride severs the tongue of a man who tries to rape her in her hospital bed where she has been in a deep coma for four years. After her miraculous recovery, she slays Copperhead, a member of Bill's gang who sought to murder her at her wedding, in a duel of revenge at Copperhead's Pasadena home, while Copperhead's daughter looks on. A male Oriental voice-over then advises The Bride that "vanquishing thy enemy can be the warrior's only concern; suppress all human emotion and compassion." This advice opposes not only the course taken by Barlow and his friends in *Three Kings*, but also Benigno's disposition at the start of *Talk to Her*. At least initially, he perfectly embodies emotion and compassion.

Talk to Her offers scant evidence that Benigno's statement to another nurse, Rosa (Mariola Fuentes), that Alicia may yet wake up—and that he believes in miracles, as should Rosa—derives from his religious beliefs. Instead, Benigno's statement may be taken as a further sign of his sheer wonder at life, his humaneness, and his fervent hope for his patient's well-being. Moreover, that he talks to Alicia about art and emotion—and presents her with a photograph she cannot see—may be unusual, but not unwise. Indeed, a recent scientific finding reported in *The New York Times* supports his approach: "A severely brain-damaged woman in an unresponsive, vegetative state showed clear signs of conscious awareness on brain imaging tests . . . in a finding that could have far-reaching consequences for how unconscious patients are cared for and diagnosed. . . . The woman was injured in a traffic accident last year." The newspaper also quotes a neurology professor at Dartmouth Medical School who was not involved in the study: "Even though we might assume some patients are not aware, I think we should always talk to them, always explain what's going on, always make them comfortable, because maybe they are there, inside, aware of everything."[36] Given that Benigno's approach to caring for Alicia may be sound, and that in any case his compassion for her is noble, where, and when, does he go wrong?

Crucial to the answer is Almodóvar's way of telling this story. Except for a few scenes— Benigno advising Rosa about miracles, conversing with Alicia's father and then Marco at the hospital, overseeing Alicia during her dance teacher's visit—he is absent much of the time following the second scene in which he touchingly tells Alicia about the Bausch concert. His obsession with Alicia before the accident, as well as his extreme isolation and his aggressive pursuit of her, are not revealed to the film's spectator until a flashback in scene nineteen highlights these actions and circumstances, including Benigno's intrusion into Alicia's home. Not only the flashback's content is unsettling, but also its form, as the narrative viewpoint within the flashback shifts from the film's director to Benigno, while the intended recipient seems at first to be the film's spectator, but then turns out to be Marco (who has joined Benigno on the hospital terrace just prior to the flashback). Further, the flashback is disturbing because the turbulent events occupying the interval between scene two and the flashback underscore how oddly ideal—how pacific and full of love, thanks largely to Benigno—scene two was. These events intervening between scene two and the flashback focus on Marco and the bullfighter Lydia (Rosario Flores), depicting not only their budding romance, but also their painful breakups with former lovers, their consequent grief and loneliness, Lydia's snake phobia, and then her near-fatal goring by a bull, leaving her in a deep coma like Alicia—and in the same hospital, where Marco and Benigno meet for the first time since their encounter in the theatre. Compared to the mishaps and torments of Marco and Lydia, the time shared by Benigno and Alicia in the hospital seems all the more golden.

Perhaps not only Benigno generates the aura of beatitude in Alicia's hospital room, but also Alicia (or what remains of her); and perhaps each of them contributes as well to the falsity of that aura. Tranquil, beautiful Alicia, appearing not the least ravaged, or even scarred, as a result of her accident, resembles at moments a sleeping princess. As Marco heads toward a meeting with Lydia's doctor, he sees Alicia semi-nude, breasts fully exposed, through the open door to her room. Suddenly her eyes open, and Marco has to catch his breath. The doctor will inform him that patients such as Lydia and Alicia open their eyes occasionally, but without seeing anything. Nevertheless, posed somewhat like Édouard Manet's nude in *Olympia* (1863), Alicia looks irresistibly sensual and alive. It seems incredible that, as Marco says later, she is "practically dead"—or, one of the living dead, a hybrid form fit for horror more than romance. Further, the aliveness Benigno experiences in caring for her depends on his fantasy that she is sentient rather than lifeless. The flashback of his first encounters with Alicia, including the one in her home, possibly alerts the film's spectator to the darkness and delusion underlying the halcyon images of the nurse and his patient in the hospital.

Paradoxes of being and non-being posed by Alicia and Benigno already intrude in the scene prior to the flashback, when Alicia's dance teacher Katerina (Geraldine Chaplin) describes to her unconscious student and Benigno a performance she is preparing in Geneva. As Katerina speaks of costumes and a blood stain, Benigno exclaims, "That's lovely. Alicia's loving it"; and as Katerina explains that the accompanying music will include Krzysztof Penderecki's *Threnody to the Victims of Hiroshima* (1959–61), Benigno says, ". . . Alicia remembers it perfectly." Later, Benigno will speak for Lydia as well, though only briefly, about the pleasure of resting on the hospital terrace on a fine day. In any case, perhaps for the first time in *Talk to Her*, Benigno, in addressing Katerina, suddenly speaks *for* Alicia and not just to her. Possibly he has talked to Alicia until now in the faint hope that she would either understand his words, or at least vaguely benefit from their tone or spirit. But now Benigno asserts without qualification that Alicia has distinct thoughts and feelings and that he knows precisely what they are. Perhaps she magically communicates them to him by means that defy detection by other individuals; or he discovers them through empathy, or by inhabiting her mind and body. The chance remains, of course, that there is nothing to enter, that no thoughts or feelings are to be discovered within Alicia, and that Benigno invents everything in the face of emptiness.

The account of hybrid cinema presented in this book has more than once focused on empathy, on the capacity to identify with the experience of others, to take in thoughts and feelings outside ourselves. Such identification entails a degree of reaching out, of merging or overlapping with others, that somewhat parallels the workings of hybrid form, in which ordinarily distinct genres, styles, and tones fuse or merge. According to this view, characters in hybrid films whose empathy takes them beyond the usual confines of their identity resemble the films they inhabit, even though films do not have feelings as people do. Empathy figures perhaps more prominently in *Talk to Her* than in any other film considered in this book. For as I have indicated, a pivotal question throughout Almodóvar's film is whether Benigno's apparently vast capacity for empathy and identification locates a suitable object, which would be, at the least, another individual who possesses distinct thoughts and feelings. Or does Benigno, in reaching or vaulting outward, merge or unite solely with his own projections or fantasies? Even though Benigno may possess a wide range of moods and tempi—somewhat as melodrama does, according to Thomas Elsaesser—for him to reach out only to find aspects of himself suggests a dead-end, a triumph of solipsism over empathy. Is *Talk to Her*, then, a mixture of tragedy, melodrama, and horror about a desperate man self-imprisoned well before society incarcerates him?

Or is it predominately a bold, comic romance about a relentlessly hopeful man, perhaps forty years old, hitherto a virgin, and with uncertain sexual preferences, who saves the woman he loves by daring to believe he can exist within her forever, and, as Marco indicates at Benigno's grave, awaken her with his love? Indeed, though the fetus is born dead, and Benigno commits suicide, Alicia regains consciousness. While unable to walk without crutches, she resumes something of her former life. Marco encounters her, after he visits Benigno's grave, at a Nina Bausch dance concert far more lilting than the one at the start of the film; and at the very instant this cheerier dance piece concludes *Talk to Her*, romance dawns between Alicia and Marco, the two individuals most beloved by Benigno in all the world—who, until now, have never really met.

Romantic, tragic Benigno is also the film's chief comedian, and comedy figures as much as any other genre in *Talk to Her*. After Benigno talks *for* Alicia, not just to her, during Katerina's visit, he shows Alicia a magazine illustration of a bedroom set, which he tells her he plans to purchase for the home they will establish in the apartment he shared with his mother. More than his speaking for Alicia, his plan for a future home with her seems not merely comical, but also ominous. Comedy stages a comeback, though, when Benigno presents himself to Marco as an authority on the feminine mystique, and the two men enter into an almost standard comic debate about the tactics of heterosexual romance. The debate quickens when Marco complains to Benigno that he cannot bear to touch Lydia, even though he has been her lover, and Benigno responds by trying to teach his friend how to relate to unconscious Lydia as effectively as Benigno relates, or so he believes, to unconscious Alicia:

Marco: I don't recognize her body. I can't even help the nurses to turn her over in the bed. And I feel so despicable.

Benigno: Talk to her. Tell her that.

Marco: I'd like to but she can't hear me.

Benigno: Why are you so sure about that?

Marco: Because her brain is turned off.

Benigno (taking Alicia's blood pressure): A woman's brain is a mystery, and in this state even more so. . . . You have to pay attention to women, talk to them, be thoughtful occasionally. Caress them. Remember they exist, they're alive and they matter to us. . . . That's the only therapy. I know from experience.

Marco (irritated, surprised): What experience have you had with women . . . ?

Benigno: What? Me? A lot. I lived twenty years day and night with one, and four years with this one.

Marco later learns that a month prior to Lydia's injury she reconciled with her previous lover, the bullfighter known as El Niño de Valencia (Adolfo Fernández), though she did not get around to telling Marco. Perhaps the journalist has been unable to touch Lydia in the hospital because he has long sensed the shift in her affection. In any case, when, shortly after receiving this news, Marco tells Benigno of his intention to travel abroad, Benigno at once senses at least part of the truth: "Have you split up?" he asks Marco. "You could say that," replies the journalist, whereupon the male nurse, as ever an expert on romance, assures him that he saw the breakup coming. "There was something in your relationship, forgive me, that didn't work." As often happens in *Talk to Her*, Benigno both hits the mark and misses it. Marco's relationship with Lydia was not working, but the failure was already under way when she and El Niño de Valencia healed their breach prior to her accident; moreover, the accident precluded, far more than Benigno has been willing to admit, emotional interaction of any sort between Lydia and Marco. Something of a saint and a savant, Benigno is also a bit of a fool. When he loses his virginity to Alicia, he becomes a criminal as well.

Almodóvar once described *Blue Velvet* as "more morbid than my films because there is always an element of naiveté in what I am doing. . . ."[37] An instance of *Talk to Her*'s complex shifting of tones and generic allusions, with comedy trumping morbidity yet laying the ground for tragedy, occurs when Benigno ventures beyond merely thinking about having sex with Alicia as he soberly describes to her the hilarious silent film, *Shrinking Lover*. He not only recounts the film, which he has just seen, but in essence replays it—its images accompany his description. The result is possibly the funniest, most exuberant sequence in all of *Talk to Her* just as *Talk to Her* takes a most tragic turn.

Shrinking Lover contributes to the generic variety of the larger film by seamlessly fusing horror and science fiction with farce. In addition, via the silent movie as narrated by Benigno, Almodóvar impishly positions silent cinema— along with the tradition of the live commentator (or *benshi*, in Japan)—at the heart of a talking motion picture that persistently ponders the value of talking as it juxtaposes Benigno's spoken words to Alicia's unwavering silence. Simultaneously, Almodóvar offers a visual pun on the convention of the film within a film: consistent with the reduced screen size of earlier motion pictures, *Shrinking Lover* occupies a diminished frame within the wide screen of *Talk to Her*; similarly, the black-and-white of *Shrinking Lover* is contained within the color of *Talk to Her*; and the speeded-up motion of the silent farce is framed by the more naturalistic pace of Benigno's world, which is going rapidly off course nonetheless.

The moment Benigno starts to tell Alicia the story of *Shrinking Lover*, he seems aroused and disturbed by the sight of Alicia's breasts—and possibly by his desire to be consumed or absorbed by her. The hero of the silent film is Alfredo, who recklessly drinks an experimental potion devised by his scientist/girlfriend, Amparo, to help people lose weight.[38] The drink enlarges Alfredo's libido, while his body shrinks until finally it is smaller than almost any item in Amparo's purse. Before fully shrinking, though, Alfredo decides to spare Amparo further sight of his decline. Looking determined but forlorn like a character in Kafka or Gogol, with luggage clutched in each hand of his dwindling frame, Alfredo departs the home in Madrid he shares with Amparo without telling her his destination. After many years, Amparo discovers he is living with his mother, a terrible person he once avoided. Amparo then journeys to his mother's home, and takes him in her purse to a hotel. In bed with Amparo, a happy, energized Alfredo encourages his weary sweetheart to close her eyes and get some rest, assuring her he will not let her accidentally crush him as she moves around. Then, when she is asleep, he climbs, tumbles, and romps nimbly over her body, kissing her here and there. Eventually he stands between her slightly spread thighs admiring her genitalia, though the entire area has turned into the inanimate surface of a mannequin. After some time probing the false vagina with his hand, and then with his entire body (he dives in head first), Alfredo finally dispenses with his underwear and enters her—or it—for good. Amparo's sleeping face glows with pleasure in close-up as she gently bites her lip. The film cuts to a close-up of Alicia's equally beautiful face, her eyes closed as usual. Benigno, in a fuller shot, strokes Alicia's legs as he completes the story: "And Alfredo . . . stays inside her . . . forever."

Not only diverse tones and genres, but also diverse identities converge in *Talk to Her*. Lydia even prior to her accident resembles at moments comatose

Alicia. Close-ups of Lydia being dressed for her near-fatal bullfight bring to mind close-ups of Alicia being helped into and out of her hospital garb and getting scrubbed and massaged. And if Alicia's lovely face resembles Amparo's, Alicia's lifelessness is remembered in Amparo's mannequin parts. As I have mentioned, Alicia also resembles somewhat the dancers with closed eyes who are attired in stark white slips; and in her physical reliance on Benigno she resembles his mother who, beautiful but lazy in his view, needed him to wash her, do her nails, and cut and dye her hair. Further, if Amparo is linked to Alicia, Alfredo resembles Benigno (and the film cuts between the two couples throughout Benigno's replay of *Shrinking Lover*). Both Benigno and Alfredo are chubby, as Benigno notes; each lives cooped up for years with his mother; and each ends his life consumed by a hopeless passion.

Probably Benigno most resembles Marco, however. Both individuals are terribly lonely. Marco talks to the unconscious Alicia just once—to tell her he is "alone again" after he learns that Lydia reconciled with her former lover without informing him. The journalist who has traveled widely and the stay-at-home nurse dedicated to Alicia become intimate friends. When Marco visits Benigno in prison, the two agree that Marco will rent Benigno's apartment, and the film's surprise ending hints that Marco may even live there as Benigno wanted to live—with Alicia. At the very instant Marco and Benigno, facing each other through a glass barrier as they converse in the prison, agree that Marco will take Benigno's apartment, reflections playing off the glass result in the superimposition of their faces. Hence these two men briefly constitute one hybrid visual image, possibly betokening not only that their needs overlap, but that they are alive to each other, that the empathy of each individual has for the moment found in the other a suitable object.

NOTES

1. Thomas Elsaesser, "Tales of Sound and Fury: Observations on the Family Melodrama," in Gerald Mast, Marshall Cohen, and Leo Braudy (eds.), *Film Theory and Criticism. Introductory Readings*, Fourth Edition (New York: Oxford University Press, 1992), p. 518.

2. Linda Hutcheon, *The Politics of Postmodernism*, Second Edition (London and New York: Routledge, 1989), p. 5.

3. Roger Ebert furnishes this information in his review of *Shaolin Soccer* on April 23, 2004.

4. *Kung Fu Hustle* grossed $17 million in the United States.

5. David Bordwell, *Planet Hong Kong. Popular Cinema and the Art of Entertainment* (Cambridge, MA: Harvard University Press, 2000), p. 1.

6. Bordwell, *Planet Hong Kong*, p. 11.

7. Bordwell, *Planet Hong Kong*, p. 9.

8. Bordwell, *Planet Hong Kong*, p. 10.

9. Howard Hampton, "Wong Kar-wai. Blur as Genre," *ARTFORUM*, Vol. 34, No. 7, March 1996, p. 92.

10. This exchange occurred in an interview with Wong Kar-wai conducted by Peter Brunette at the Toronto International Film Festival in 1995. See Peter Brunette, *Wong Kar-wai* (Urbana and Chicago: University of Illinois Press, 2005), p. 117.

11. Elvis Mitchell, review of *Shaolin Soccer*, *New York Times*, April 2, 2004.

12. Manohla Dargis, "Politics Arch and Subtle at Toronto Film Festival," *New York Times*, September 14, 2006.

13. André Bazin, *What Is Cinema? Vol. II*, trans. Hugh Gray (Berkeley: University of California Press, 1971), pp. 81–82.

14. Georges Sadoul, *Dictionary of Films*, translated, edited, and updated by Peter Morris (Berkeley: University of California Press, 1972), p. 389.

15. Janet Maslin, review of *Run Lola Run*, *New York Times*, March 26, 1999.

16. See, for example, Ulrich Niemann, "In Focus," *Korea Times*, June 28, 2002.

17. A. O. Scott, review of *Talk to Her*, *New York Times*, November 17, 2002.

18. Lynn Hirschberg, "The Redeemer," *New York Times Magazine*, September 5, 2004, p. 26.

19. Hirschberg, "The Redeemer," p. 43.

20. Quoted in Paula Willoquet-Maricondi (ed.), *Pedro Almodóvar Interviews* (Jackson: University Press of Mississippi, 2004), p. 48. From "Pleasure and the New Spanish Morality: A Conversation with Pedro Almodóvar," by Marsha Kinder in *Film Quarterly*, Fall 1987.

21. Hirschberg, "The Redeemer," p. 38.

22. Willoquet-Maricondi, *Pedro Almodóvar Interviews*, p. 47; from interview by Marsha Kinder.

23. Michael Wood, *BELLE DE JOUR* (London: British Film Institute, 2005), p. 46.

24. Willoquet-Maricondi, *Pedro Almodóvar Interviews*, p. ix.

25. Willoquet-Maricondi, *Pedro Almodóvar Interviews*, p. 141. From an interview with Almodóvar by Guillermo Altares published in *Positif*, Vol. 460, in 1999.

26. Willoquet-Maricondi, *Pedro Almodóvar Interviews*, p. 47; interview by Kinder.

27. Willoquet-Maricondi, *Pedro Almodóvar Interviews*, p. 140; interview by Altares.

28. Hirschberg, "The Redeemer," p. 24.

29. Willoquet-Maricondi, *Pedro Almodóvar Interviews*, p. 54; interview by Kinder.

30. Willoquet-Maricondi, *Pedro Almodóvar Interviews*, p. 141; interview by Altares.

31. Willoquet-Maricondi, *Pedro Almodóvar Interviews*, p. 50; interview by Kinder.

32. Willoquet-Maricondi, *Pedro Almodóvar Interviews*, p. 142; interview by Altares.

33. Willoquet-Maricondi, *Pedro Almodóvar Interviews*, p. 147; interview by Altares.

34. Willoquet-Maricondi, *Pedro Almodóvar Interviews*, p. xiii.

35. Willoquet-Maricondi, *Pedro Almodóvar Interviews*, p. 147; interview by Altares.

36. Benedict Carey, "Vegetative Patient Shows Signs of Awareness, Study Says," *New York Times*, September 7, 2006.

37. Willoquet-Maricondi, *Pedro Almodóvar Interviews*, p. 47; interview by Kinder.

38. Fele Martínez plays Alfredo, while Paz Vega is Amparo.

Selected Bibliography

Alea, Tomás Gutiérrez and Edmundo Desnoes. *Memories of Underdevelopment and Inconsolable Memories*. New Brunswick, NJ: Rutgers University Press, 1990.

Altares, Guillermo. "An Act of Love toward Oneself." In *Pedro Almodóvar Interviews*, edited by Paula Willoquet-Maricondi, 139–154. Jackson: University Press of Mississippi, 2004.

Altman, Rick. *Film/Genre*. London: British Film Institute, 2006.

Andrew, Geoff. *Stranger than paradise. Maverick film-makers in recent American cinema*. New York: Limelight, 1999.

Appiah, Kwame Anthony. *Cosmopolitanism: Ethics in a World of Strangers*. New York: W.W. Norton, 2006.

Armes, Roy. *Patterns of Realism*. New York: A.S. Barnes & Co., 1971.

Bakhtin, M.M. *The Dialogic Imagination. Four Essays*, edited by Michael Holquist and translated by Caryl Emerson and Michael Holquist. Austin: University of Texas Press, 1981.

Barnouw, Erik. *Documentary. A History of the Non-Fiction Film*, Second Revised Edition. New York: Oxford University Press, 1993.

Baudrillard, Jean. *The Gulf War Did Not Take Place*. Trans. Paul Patton. Bloomington: Indiana University Press, 1995.

Bazin, André. *What Is Cinema? Vol. II.* Trans. Hugh Gray. Berkeley: University of California Press, 1971.

Beaver, Frank E. *Dictionary of Film Terms.* New York: McGraw-Hill, 1983.

Bentley, Eric. *The Life of the Drama.* New York: Atheneum, 1970.

Boorstin, Daniel J. *THE IMAGE. A Guide to Pseudo-Events in America.* New York: Vintage, 1987.

Bordwell, David. *Planet Hong Kong. Popular Cinema and the Art of Entertainment.* Cambridge, MA: Harvard University Press, 2000.

Brakhage, Stan. *Metaphors on Vision.* New York: Film Culture, 1963.

Brooks, Peter. *The Melodramatic Imagination. Balzac, Henry James, Melodrama, and the Mode of Excess.* New York: Columbia University Press, 1985.

Browne, Nick, ed. *Refiguring American Film Genres. History and Theory.* Berkeley: University of California Press, 1998.

Brunette, Peter. *Wong Kar-wai.* Urbana and Chicago: University of Illinois Press, 2005.

Bryson, Bill. *A Short History of Nearly Everything.* New York: Broadway Books, 2003.

Buñuel, Luis. *My Last Sigh.* Trans. Abigail Israel. New York: Vintage, 1984.

Burgess, Anthony. *English Literature. A Survey for Students.* London: Longman, 1974.

Cameron, Ian and Robin Wood. *Antonioni.* New York: Praeger, 1968.

Chion, Michael. *David Lynch.* Trans. Robert Julian. London: British Film Institute, 1995.

Coen, Ethan and Joel. *FARGO.* London: Faber and Faber, 2000.

Crary, Jonathan. "Spectacle." In *New Keywords. A Revised Vocabulary of Culture and Society,* edited by Tony Bennett, Lawrence Grossberg, and Meaghan Morris, 335–36. Malden, MA: Blackwell, 2005.

Danner, Mark. "What Are You Going to Do with That?" *New York Review of Books* LII, no. 11 (June 23, 2005): 52–56.

Dargis, Manohla. "Quentin Tarantino on *Pulp Fiction.*" In *American Independent Cinema. A Sight and Sound Reader,* edited by Jim Hillier, 240–45. London: British Film Institute, 2001.

Dixon, Wheeler Winston, ed. *Film Genre 2000. New Critical Essays.* Albany: State University of New York Press, 2000.

Eisenstein, Sergei. "A Dialectic Approach to Film Form." In *Film Form and Film Sense*, edited and translated by Jay Leyda, 45–64. Cleveland: Meridian, 1964.

Eliot, T.S. *The Complete Poems and Plays 1909–1950*. New York: Harcourt Brace, 1980.

Elsaesser, Thomas. "Tales of Sound and Fury: Observations on the Family Melodrama." In *Film Theory and Criticism. Introductory Readings*, Fourth Edition, edited by Gerald Mast, Marshall Cohen, and Leo Braudy, 512–36. New York: Oxford University Press, 1992.

Ernst, Max. *UNE SEMAINE DE BONTÉ. A Surrealistic Novel in Collage*. New York: Dover, 1976.

Esslin, Martin. *The Theatre of the Absurd*. New York: Anchor, 1969.

Farber, Manny. *Movies*. New York: Hillstone, 1985.

Gledhill, Christine, ed. *Home Is Where the Heart Is. Studies in Melodrama and the Woman's Film*. London: British Film Institute, 1971.

Godard, Jean-Luc. *Godard on Godard*. Translated with commentary by Tom Milne. New York: Viking, 1972.

———. *Weekend/Wind from the East*. Trans. Marianne Sinclair. New York: Simon and Schuster, 1972.

Grant, Barry Keith, ed. *Film Genre Reader* III. Austin: University of Texas Press, 2003.

Hampton, Howard. "Wong Kar-wai. Blur as Genre." *ARTFORUM* 34, no. 7 (March 1996): 90–93.

Haynes, Todd. *Far from Heaven, Safe, Superstar: The Karen Carpenter Story. Three Screenplays*. New York: Grove Press, 2003.

Hayward, Susan. *Cinema Studies: The Key Concepts*, Second Edition. London and New York: Routledge, 2000.

Hillier, Jim, ed. *American Independent Cinema. A Sight and Sound Reader*. London: British Film Institute, 2001.

Holquist, Michael. "Introduction." In *The Dialogic Imagination. Four Essays by M.M. Bakhtin*, edited by Michael Holquist and translated by Caryl Emerson and Michael Holquist, xv–xxxiii. Austin: University of Texas Press, 1981.

Hutcheon, Linda. *The Politics of Postmodernism*, Second Edition. London and New York: Routledge, 1989.

Jaffe, Ira. "Errol Morris's Forms of Control." *Film International* 14, no. 2 (2005): 4–19.

Kagan, Norman. *The Cinema of Stanley Kubrick.* New York: Grove Press, 1972.

Keyssar, Helene. *Robert Altman's America.* New York: Oxford University Press, 1991.

Kinder, Marsha. "Pleasure and the New Spanish Morality. A Conversation with Pedro Almodóvar." In *Pedro Almodóvar Interviews*, edited by Paula Willoquet-Maricondi, 40–58. Jackson: University Press of Mississippi, 2004.

Klawans, Stuart. "The Avengers." *The Nation* (November 10, 2003): 31–34.

Klinger, Barbara. *Melodrama and Meaning. History, Culture, and the Films of Douglas Sirk.* Bloomington: Indiana University Press, 1994.

Kolker, Robert. *A Cinema of Loneliness*, Third Edition. New York: Oxford University Press, 2000.

Kostelanetz, Richard. *John Cage (ex)plain(ed).* New York: Schirmer, 1996.

Kracauer, Siegfried. *From Caligari to Hitler. A Psychological History of the German Film.* Princeton, NJ: Princeton University Press, 1947.

———. *Theory of Film. The Redemption of Physical Reality.* New York: Oxford University Press, 1960.

Langer, Susanne K. "A Note on the Film." In *Feeling and Form*, by Susanne K. Langer, 411–15. New York: Charles Scribner's Sons, 1953.

Langford, Barry. *Film Genre. Hollywood and Beyond.* Edinburgh: Edinburgh University Press, 2005.

Leyda, Jay. *KINO. A History of Russian and Soviet Film.* New York: Macmillan, 1960.

Linklater, Richard. *Slacker.* New York: St. Martin's Press, 1992.

Lynch, David. *Lynch on Lynch.* Edited by Chris Rodley. London: Faber and Faber, 1997.

MacFarquhar, Larissa. "The Movie Lover." *New Yorker* (October 20, 2003): 147–59.

Maltby, Richard. *Hollywood Cinema. An Introduction.* Oxford, UK and Malden, MA: Blackwell, 1999.

Marcus, Millicent. *Italian Film in the Light of Neorealism.* Princeton, NJ: Princeton University Press, 1986.

Matthiessen, F.O. *The Achievement of T.S. Eliot. An Essay on the Nature of Poetry.* New York: Oxford University Press, 1959.

Mendelsohn, Daniel. "It's Only a Movie." *New York Review of Books* L, no. 20 (December 18, 2003): 38–41.

Michelson, Annette. "Introduction." In Nagisa Oshima, *Cinema, Censorship, and the State: The Writings of Nagisa Oshima, 1956–1978*, edited by Annette Michelson and translated by Dawn Lawson, 1–6. Cambridge, MA: MIT Press, 1992.

Miller, Arthur. *On Politics and the Art of Acting*. New York: Viking, 2001.

Morgan, Robert P., ed. *Music Society and Modern Times. From World War I to the present*. Englewood Cliffs, NJ: Prentice Hall, 1994.

Münsterberg, Hugo. "Excerpt from *The Film: A Psychological Study*." In *Film Theory and Criticism. Introductory Readings*, Fifth Edition, edited by Leo Braudy and Marshall Cohen, 401–408. New York: Oxford University Press, 1999.

Neale, Steve. *Genre and Hollywood*. London and New York: Routledge, 2005.

Nichols, Bill. *Introduction to Documentary*. Bloomington: Indiana University Press, 2001.

Oja, Carol J. "The USA, 1918–45." In *Music Society and Modern Times. From World War I to the present*, edited by Robert P. Morgan, 206–31. Englewood Cliffs, NJ: Prentice Hall, 1994.

Palmer, R. Barton. *Joel and Ethan Coen*. Urbana and Chicago: University of Illinois Press, 2004.

Pavlus, John. "A Bride Vows Vengeance." *American Cinematographer* 84, no. 10 (October 2003): 33–47.

Pierson, John. *SPIKE, MIKE, SLACKERS & DYKES. A Guided Tour Across a Decade of American Independent Cinema*. New York: Hyperion Miramax, 1995.

Polan, Dana. *Pulp Fiction*. London: British Film Institute, 2000.

Posner, Richard A. "Bad News." *New York Times Book Review* (July 31, 2005): 1, 8–11.

Pratt, George C. *Spellbound in Darkness. A History of Silent Film*. Greenwich, CT: New York Graphic Society Ltd., 1973.

Robbe-Grillet, Alain. *Last Year at Marienbad*. Trans. Richard Howard. New York: Grove Press, 1962.

Rothman, William. *Documentary Film Classics*. New York: Cambridge University Press, 1997.

Sadoul, Georges. *Dictionary of Films*. Translated, edited, and updated by Peter Morris. Berkeley: University of California Press, 1972.

Sarris, Andrew. *YOU AIN'T HEARD NOTHIN' YET. The American Talking Film. History and Memory 1927–1949*. New York: Oxford University Press, 1998.

Scott, A. O. "The Track of a Teardrop, a Filmmaker's Path." In *Pedro Almodóvar Interviews*, edited by Paula Willoquet-Maricondi, 162–67. Jackson: University Press of Mississippi, 2004. First published in *New York Times* (November 17, 2002).

Sitney, P. Adams. *Visionary Film. The American Avant-Garde 1943–2000*, Third Edition. New York: Oxford University Press, 2002.

Sontag, Susan. *Against Interpretation*. New York: Delta, 1966.

Stevens, Wallace. *The Necessary Angel. Essays on Reality and Imagination*. New York: Vintage, 1951.

Tarantino, Quentin. *Pulp Fiction. A Quentin Tarantino Screenplay*. New York: Miramax, 1994.

Telford, Kenneth A. *Aristotle's Poetics: Translation and Analysis*. Chicago: Henry Regenery Company, 1961.

Tomkins, Calvin. *Off the Wall. Robert Rauschenberg and the Art World of Our Time*. New York: Penguin, 1985.

Turim, Maureen. *The Films of Oshima Nagisa. Images of a Japanese Iconoclast*. Berkeley: University of California Press, 1998.

Venturi, Robert. *Complexity and Contradiction in Architecture*. New York: Museum of Modern Art, 1979.

Vertov, Dziga. *KINO-EYE. The Writings of Dziga Vertov*. Translated by Kevin O'Brien and edited by Annette Michelson. Berkeley: University of California Press, 1984.

Williams, Linda. "Melodrama Revised." In *Refiguring American Film Genres. History and Theory*, edited by Nick Browne, 42–89. Berkeley: University of California Press, 1998.

Wood, Michael. *BELLE DE JOUR*. London: British Film Institute, 2005.

Selected Filmography

UNITED STATES

Life of an American Fireman (1902, E.S. Porter)

The Great Train Robbery (1903, Porter)

Intolerance (1916, D. W. Griffith)

Nanook of the North (1922, Robert Flaherty)

Duck Soup (1933, Leo McCarey)

Forty-Second Street (1933, Lloyd Bacon & Busby Berkeley)

Gold Diggers of 1933 (1933, Mervyn LeRoy & Busby Berkeley)

The Great Dictator (1940, Charlie Chaplin)

Meshes of the Afternoon (1943, Maya Deren)

Monsieur Verdoux (1947, Chaplin)

Singin' in the Rain (1951, Gene Kelly & Stanley Donen)

All that Heaven Allows (1956, Douglas Sirk)

The Three Faces of Eve (1957, Nunnally Johnson)

A Movie (1958, Bruce Conner)

Dr. Strangelove. Or How I Learned to Stop Worrying and Love the Bomb (1964, Stanley Kubrick)

Dog Star Man (1961–64, Stan Brakhage)

Report (1964, Conner)

Nashville (1975, Robert Altman)

Hearts and Minds (1975, Peter Davis)

3 Women (1977, Altman)

The Atomic Café (1982, Kevin Rafferty, Jayne Loader, & Pierce Rafferty)

Come Back to the Five and Dime, Jimmy Dean, Jimmy Dean (1982, Altman)

Paris, Texas (1984, Wim Wenders)

Blue Velvet (1986, David Lynch)

The Thin Blue Line (1989, Errol Morris)

Poison (1991, Todd Haynes)

Slacker (1991, Richard Linklater)

Pulp Fiction (1994, Quentin Tarantino)

Fargo (1996, Ethan and Joel Coen)

Fast, Cheap and Out of Control (1997, Morris)

Lost Highway (1997, Lynch)

The Truman Show (1998, Peter Weir)

Best in Show (1999, Christopher Guest)

Fight Club (1999, David Fincher)

Mr. Death: The Rise and Fall of Fred A. Leuchter, Jr. (1999, Morris)

Three Kings (1999, David O. Russell)

Memento (2000, Christopher Nolan)

Mulholland Drive (2001, Lynch)

Bowling for Columbine (2002, Michael Moore)

Far from Heaven (2002, Haynes)

Bright Leaves (2003, Ross McElwee)

Capturing the Friedmans (2003, Andrew Jarecki)

The Fog of War: Eleven Lessons from the Life of Robert S. McNamara (2003, Morris)

Kill Bill: Vol. 1 (2003, Tarantino)

Fahrenheit 9/11 (2004, Moore)

Kill Bill: Vol. 2 (2004, Tarantino)

Tarnation (2004, Jonathan Caouette)

Broken Flowers (2005, Jim Jarmusch)

OTHER COUNTRIES

Trip to the Moon (1902, Georges Méliès)

The Cabinet of Dr. Caligari (1919, Robert Weine)

Return to Reason (1921, Man Ray)

Entr'acte (1924, René Clair)

The Last Laugh (1924, F.W. Murnau)

Strike (1924, Sergei Eisenstein)

Zvenigora (1927, Alexandre Dovzhenko)

October (1927–28, Eisenstein)

The Man with a Movie Camera (1929, Dziga Vertov)

Un Chien andalou (1929, Luis Buñuel & Salvador Dalí)

Rules of the Game (1939, Jean Renoir)

Umberto D (1951, Vittorio De Sica)

Tokyo Story (1953, Yasujiro Ozu)

Breathless (1959, Jean-Luc Godard)

Last Year at Marienbad (1961, Alain Resnais & Alain Robbe-Grillet)

Persona (1966, Ingmar Bergman)

Belle de Jour (1967, Buñuel)

Weekend (1967, Godard)

The Hour of the Furnaces (1968, Fernando Solanas & Octavio Getino)

Lucía (1968, Humberto Solas)

Memories of Underdevelopment (1968, Tomás Gutiérrez Alea)

Death by Hanging (1969, Nagisa Oshima)

The Jackal of Nahueltoro (1969, Miguel Littín)

Fear Eats the Soul (1974, Rainer Werner Fassbinder)

The Marriage of Maria Braun (1979, Fassbinder)

Chungking Express (1994, Wong Kar-wai)

Live Flesh (1997, Pedro Almodóvar)

Run Lola Run (1998, Tom Tykwer)

All about My Mother (1999, Almodóvar)

The Princess and the Warrior (2001, Tykwer)

Shaolin Soccer (2001, Stephen Chow)

Talk to Her (2002, Almodóvar)

Notre Musique (2004, Godard)

The World (2004, Jia Zhang-ke)

Kung Fu Hustle (2005, Chow)

Index

About the Author

Ira Jaffe is professor emeritus and former chair of the Department of Media Arts at the University of New Mexico. He is also a former presidential lecturer and associate dean in UNM's College of Fine Arts, which he joined after teaching at the University of Southern California School of Cinema. He is coeditor of *Redirecting the Gaze: Gender, Theory, and Cinema in the Third World,* and author of essays about Robert Altman, Charlie Chaplin, Errol Morris, and Orson Welles. His writing appears in *Perspectives on Citizen Kane* and *Hollywood as Historian: American Film in a Cultural Context,* as well as in periodicals including *ARTSPACE, Film International,* and *Film Quarterly.* He founded at UNM the International Cinema Lecture Series and Latin American Film Festival as well as the Department of Media Arts.

Washington County Free Library
100 South Potomac Street
Hagerstown, MD 21740-5504
www.washcolibrary.org

3 2395 00809 7798